COMMUNION: THE MEAL THAT UNITES?

By the same authors:

SPIRITUAL GIFTS AND THE CHURCH,
published by Inter-Varsity Press

THE WATER THAT DIVIDES,
published by Inter-Varsity Press

Communion: The Meal That Unites?

Donald Bridge &
David Phypers

Harold Shaw Publishers
Wheaton, Illinois

The Meal That Unites? © 1981 by Donald Bridge and David Phypers

All rights reserved. No part of this book may be reproduced or transmitted in any form or by any means, electronic or mechanical, including photcopying, recording, or any information storage and retrieval system without written permission from Harold Shaw Publishers, Box 567, Wheaton, Illinois 60189

Communion: The Meal That Unites? is printed in the United States of America by special arrangement with Hodder & Stoughton, Ltd., England.

Library of Congress Catalog Card Number 82-62820

ISBN 0-87788-545-1

First Printing, January 1983

ACKNOWLEDGEMENTS

This book began its life as an academic dissertation, *Eucharistic Faith and Practice in History*, written by David Phypers during his training for the Church of England ministry at Lincoln Theological College. For all the help afforded by the College staff at that time the authors are most grateful, particularly for the wise oversight exercised by the Revd Dr Kenneth W. Stevenson, part-time tutor at the College and now Anglican Chaplain to the University of Manchester. David is also grateful for the help given in many conversations and lectures during that period, and in particular for interviews granted by Lord Ramsey, formerly Archbishop of Canterbury, Revd Dr Jean M. R. Tillard, Professor of Theology at the University of Ontario, Canada and member of the Anglican-Roman Catholic International Commission, and Revd Thomas A. Smail, formerly Director of the Fountain Trust and now Assistant Principal at St John's College, Nottingham.

The original dissertation has been completely rewritten by both authors together, with extensive material, particularly on the contribution of the Free Churches and the Brethren movement to eucharistic understanding, added by Donald Bridge. He is grateful to Mrs Jill Edwards and Mrs Beryl Belcher for help with typewriting. The authors are also grateful to Mrs Rosalind Doig for her final reading and correction of the proofs, and for her compilation of the index.

Needless to say, the authors are fully responsible for the views expressed in the book, and offer apologies for any mistakes which remain in the text.

FRINTON-ON-SEA, ESSEX   SUNNYHILL, DERBY
                                          SEPTEMBER 1980

CONTENTS

Introduction	9
1 – The Last Supper	13
2 – The Work of Christ	32
3 – Tribulation and Triumph	46
4 – Transubstantiation and All That	69
5 – Reformation and Division	87
6 – Evangelicals, Tractarians and Plymouth Brethren	123
7 – Twentieth-century Renewal	142
8 – Current Issues	166
Select Bibliography	187
Index	191

INTRODUCTION

Mr Average Viewer, bored with the repeat showing of a long-running television soap-opera, switches over to the slightly more sophisticated channel. To his dismay he now seems to be watching the opening sequences of a religious programme. He vaguely recalls some advance publicity; a popular star has turned his mind to twenty centuries of Christian history and proposes to enlighten the public with the results, aided by all the wizardry of modern visual and sound technology. The technology is in full flow now, and the Viewer finds his curiosity aroused. In rapid sequences of vivid colour, cunning camera angles and contrasting music, he sees brief glimpses of a string of religious ceremonies which seem to have nothing in common.

There is rich ceremonial in a Russian church where there seem to be as many priests as people, almost completely hidden by big black hats and matching beards. The throb of drums introduces a West Indian Pentecostal celebration which seems to be indistinguishable from a pop festival. Arabs in flowing robes stamp their feet in a closed circle. The good old familiar Church of England appears momentarily, in the shape of a surpliced vicar with the regulation adam's apple and tendency to adenoids. An American evangelist in tuxedo and loud tie invokes the aid of electronic organ, syrupy choir and a cross in changing psychedelic colours. Gentle-faced Asians squat in a circle and sway to the strains of odd-sounding music. The commentator, smooth, scrupulously neutral or slightly cynical, feeds in a few facts in a voice that seems to say, "Don't blame me; I'm just standing beside you, watching it."

If our Viewer has rather more than average perspicacity, he may notice the one thing the oddly different groups do have in common. They all make rather special use of bread and wine. The use they make of it is bewilderingly different, but they all use it. If he sticks with the programme for a few weeks he will soon discover that Christians have not only done different things with the bread and wine, but have done terrible things to each other because of it. Men and women have been imprisoned, whipped, pilloried, tortured, and burned alive because of differing opinions about what really happens when Christians eat bread and drink wine and remember their Lord.

Jenny Geddes has become a Scottish folk-heroine by virtue of the fact that she threw a stool at a bishop's head and shouted, "Ye'll no' say mass in ma' lug." Brave men have stood in a hostile court with their lives literally hanging on their reply to the question, "What happens to the bread and wine at the moment of consecration?" Powerful kings have been toppled from their thrones and humble men have been driven into exile because of their views about the Lord's Supper. Even today, when Christians are more conscious of their common faith than they have been for centuries, differences in eucharistic faith and practice continue to divide them. Many refuse to recognise the validity of others' celebrations. Some still withhold communion from those not in their own particular tradition.

Yet all trace their practice back to the fact that the evening before his death Jesus shared a final meal with his disciples. During the meal he said of the bread, "This is my body," and of the wine, "This is my blood." He commanded his followers, as often as they ate and drank thereafter, to remember him. As a result, the "breaking of bread", sharing in "communion", celebration of the "eucharist", partaking of "the Lord's Supper" and observance of "mass" have distinguished Christian communities ever since. They have quarrelled so deeply about its meaning because they so unitedly insist on its great importance.

At first sight Christ's actions and command seem so simple and straightforward that disagreement over their meaning and observance would appear to be impossible or merely perverse. But closer examination reveals that every action and every phrase is alive with meaning and vibrant with implication. This book is offered as a contribution to current eucharistic debate about those meanings and implications. Through a re-examination of the Biblical material and a survey of its application (and misapplication?) in history, the authors hope to present and clarify current issues. Their concern is to unite Christians and not divide them. Christians will worship in unity in the age to come, for ever. Christ and his apostles clearly regarded the eucharist as, amongst other things, a symbol and foretaste of that unity in the here-and-now.

Throughout this book, the term *eucharist* will generally be used to describe the Lord's Supper. The choice of word does not indicate any particular theological stance on the part of the authors, but has been chosen as the most neutral of the terms available. It simply means "thanksgiving", is drawn from the fact that the Supper was instituted with the giving of thanks, and has the advantage over other terms of possessing an adjective "eucharistic".

CHAPTER 1 — THE LAST SUPPER

The ancient city of Jerusalem was agog with tension and excitement. It was the time of the Passover Festival. Thousands upon thousands of Jews from every corner of the then known world had crammed into every available inch of accommodation within its walls and overspilled into seemingly endless campsites on the hills outside. For Passover was the annual commemoration of the birth of the Jewish nation. God's mighty acts as described in the Book of Exodus, whereby he protected his people from the angel of death and delivered them from slavery in Egypt, would be re-enacted in hundreds of thousands of families and groups of friends as countless Passover lambs would be slaughtered in the Jewish Temple and then roasted and eaten in solemn remembrance of that fateful night long ago.

The Festival, however, was not an altogether joyous occasion. The once proud nation of Israel which, under David and Solomon, had enjoyed worldwide power and influence was now a mere province of the mighty Roman Empire, and an exceedingly troublesome one at that. Jewish nationalism died hard. Fanned by the expectation of a Deliverer, or Messiah, who in the popular mind would repulse the Roman legions once and for all and restore the mighty kingdom of David, Jewish aspirations often flared during Passover into scenes of bloody confrontation with the Roman garrison, strengthened each year to keep the peace during these volatile days.

To the Passover came Jesus with his disciples. They had come to believe he was the long-promised Messiah, although they still thought of him as a political rather than a spiritual deliverer. At first, as Jesus rode in triumph into Jerusalem, acclaimed by eager, excited pilgrims like themselves, the disciples' hopes were raised, but during the week that followed things seemed to go from bad to worse. Not only were Jesus' claims rejected by the Jewish leaders; they actively plotted to have him killed. Finally, Judas Iscariot lost his patience. Disenchanted with Jesus' failure to organise resistance against the Romans, Judas agreed to betray him. On the night he was betrayed Jesus ate his final meal before his death with his disciples. Elements of that Last Supper have become enshrined in every form of Christian eucharist ever since. With the exception of the Quakers and the Salvation Army, all Christians everywhere, from Orthodox to Pentecostals, from Roman Catholics to Plymouth Brethren, and from the burgeoning denominations of the Third World to the independent churches and house groups of the West, celebrate that eucharist in one form or another. For many, the eucharist is integral to their life, being almost the only way in which they ever worship God. For many more, it is profoundly important and its regular celebration is the mark of their ongoing discipleship to Jesus Christ. For a few it is peripheral but still part, even if only an occasional part, of their pattern of worship.

a — Passover Feast or Fellowship Meal?

What kind of a meal was this Last Supper which Jesus ate with his disciples? The Gospels according to Matthew, Mark and Luke are quite clear. It was the Passover feast itself which Jesus reinterpreted at crucial points and applied to himself as the new Passover lamb.[1] The Gospel according to John, however, is not so clear. It seems to suggest that the Last Supper was eaten on the night before the Passover festival began, for the following morning the Jewish leaders refused to enter the Roman praetorium in Jerusalem, "so that they might not be defiled, but might eat the passover" (John 18:28). This has led many scholars to conclude that the Last Supper was a fellowship-meal such as was often eaten by groups of Jewish friends like Jesus and his disciples.[2] The verse from John could, of course, refer to "the rest of the passover" as the festival lasted for seven days after the initial meal was eaten. Thus the fourth Gospel need not contradict the other three at this point. Either way, the Last Supper was closely associated with the Passover, and an understanding of the meaning of the festival, both in its origins in the Old Testament, and in the way it was celebrated during the first century, will throw light on the meaning of Jesus' words during the meal.

b — *"This is my body. . . . This is my blood."*

The New Testament contains four accounts of the Last Supper in which Jesus' words during the meal are recorded. These accounts are in each of the first three Gospels and in Paul's First Letter to the Corinthians. The Corinthians account is generally considered to have been written first, with the Lukan account being a development of it. The Markan account is thought to have been written second, with the Matthaean one being a development of that. (In the fourth Gospel all reference to Jesus' words during the Supper is omitted; the author concentrates on Jesus' washing of his disciples' feet before the meal and on conversation about Judas Iscariot later on.)

All four accounts of the Last Supper describe how, during the meal, Jesus took bread, blessed, broke and gave it to his disciples saying, "This is my body." All add that later in the meal he took a cup of wine, passed it round and said, "This is my blood of the covenant," or, "This is the new covenant in my blood."[3]

More ink has been spilled and, sadly, more blood has been shed over the meaning of these words than over any other words in the whole of the Bible. Generally, and very broadly speaking, Orthodox and Catholic thought, for the last thousand years at least, has insisted that these words should be understood literally. Fundamental to their position has been the assertion that, in the eucharist, in some way and in some sense, the bread and wine become the actual body and blood of Christ. Equally generally, and equally very broadly speaking, this view was rejected to a greater or lesser extent by Protestants during the Reformation in the sixteenth century. On the whole, they adopted the view that Christ's words about the bread and wine at the Last Supper should be understood figuratively. In the last four hundred years thousands, possibly millions, of both Catholics and Protestants have died rather than retract their fiercely-held positions.

Significantly, however, at the Last Supper, Jesus said neither of the phrases which developed Catholic and Protestant theology really requires him to have said. He did not say, "This has become my body," nor did he say, "This represents my body." He simply said, "This is my body." Indeed, if the Greek words of the New Testament are translated into Aramaic, Jesus' native language, he probably said merely, "This my body." So what, then, did Jesus mean?

If the Last Supper was a Passover meal, then Jesus' words about the bread and wine were added to the regular words of worship which accompanied the various courses of the meal. They were added before and after the main course respectively. Between Jesus' utterances about the bread and wine the roasted Passover lamb itself, slaughtered earlier in the afternoon, was eaten. The impact of Jesus' words on his disciples could not have been more dramatic.

The original Passover lambs in Exodus had protected the people of Israel from the wrath of God, for when God had passed through the land of Egypt to destroy the firstborn, he had "passed over" the homes of the Israelites where the blood of the lambs was splashed around the doors. The original lambs brought freedom and deliverance from the slavery of Egypt. For as the Passover night wore on, the long-awaited liberation was granted. The order to go was received, and the Israelites marched in triumph from the land which had held them captive for so long. These lambs marked the beginning of a series of events in which the Israelites became a nation, the people of God. The Red Sea, Sinai and the conquest of Canaan, would bring those events to a conclusion, but the Passover lambs marked the start of them all.

The annual Passover lambs provided a constant reminder of God's mighty acts whereby he had rescued Israel from slavery and made them his own. But now, immediately before and after the lamb is eaten, Jesus says, "This is my body which is given for you. . . . This is my blood of the covenant which is poured out for many." No longer are his followers to look to the Passover and Exodus for their standing before God. They are to look to him. As Paul says, Christ is our paschal lamb, who has been sacrificed (1 Corinthians 5:7). He now protects from the wrath of God. He brings forgiveness, freedom and release. In him, members of the Christian church are constituted the people of God.

THE LAST SUPPER

There was only ever one Passover, the one described in the Book of Exodus. By their very nature, the events of that night could never be repeated. But lest they should be forgotten, God required the observance of many Passovers, "throughout your generations, as an ordinance for ever" (Exodus 12:17). Year by year, the events of Passover night were re-enacted, as the Jews gathered in Jerusalem, slaughtered the lambs and ate their meals together. The Passover lamb which Jesus and his disciples ate was thus a symbol of those first lambs which were eaten in Egypt so long ago. But so vivid was the symbol that it could be called by the reality it symbolised and treated as such. As Jesus and his disciples and all the other Jews in Jerusalem ate their Passover lambs, they could almost hear the cries of the Egyptians and the command to escape. What had happened once seemed to be happening again.

There was only ever one cross on which Jesus died, one death he died for all. By their very nature, the events of Calvary can never be repeated. But lest his followers should ever forget the cost of their redemption, Jesus required them to break bread and drink wine, "in remembrance of me." "As often as you do it," he said, "remember me." So the broken bread symbolises his broken body on the cross, the cup of wine his outpoured blood. And so vivid are the symbols that they can be called by the reality they signify, the body and blood of Christ. Again, and again, as the bread is broken and the wine poured out, Christians are intended to see their dying and bleeding Lord.

Reality or figure of speech? Faced with such a question, familiar with the Passover lamb and many, many other instances in the Old Testament where a prophet took a visual aid and called it by what it signified, the disciples of Jesus would have been quite bewildered. Both, they would have had to reply. The bread and wine are symbols, but they are also Christ's body and Christ's blood.

c — *The Bread of Life*

If the fourth Gospel is unusual in omitting Jesus' words over the bread and the wine at the Last Supper it is not generally considered to be devoid of eucharistic material. The sixth chapter records Jesus' feeding of the five thousand and goes on to describe a long discourse between Jesus, the Jews and Jesus' disciples arising out of the miracle. Jesus claims to be "the living bread which came down from heaven; if any one eats of this bread he will live for ever; and the bread which I shall give for the life of the world is my flesh.... Truly, truly, I say to you, unless you eat the flesh of the Son of man and drink his blood, you have no life in you; he who eats my flesh and drinks my blood has eternal life, and I will raise him up at the last day. For my flesh is food indeed, and my blood is drink indeed. He who eats my flesh and drinks my blood abides in me, and I in him. As the living Father sent me, and I live because of the Father, so he who eats me will live because of me. This is the bread which came down from heaven... he who eats this bread will live for ever" (John 6:51, 53-58).

From the very earliest times Christians saw a connection between this chapter and Jesus' words at the Last Supper. If the bread there was his body and the wine was his blood what more obvious way could there be of eating Christ's flesh and drinking his blood than by regularly participating in the eucharist? As the idea gained ground that, somehow, in the eucharist, the bread and wine were changed into the body and blood of Christ, so it seemed obvious that participating in the eucharist was the way to eternal life. Although Catholic theologians never lost sight of the need for faith among eucharistic worshippers, among the people this aspect came to be largely forgotten, until, by the end of the Middle Ages, mere attendance at mass, let alone receiving the elements, was popularly considered to guarantee eternal life.

Predictably, at the Reformation, Protestants reacted against this crudely literal understanding of John 6 with its promise of automatic bestowal of life merely through attendance at a service without any evidence of faith or godliness in the lives of the worshippers. They stressed verse 63, "It is the spirit that gives life, the flesh is of no avail; the words that I have spoken to you are spirit and life," and as with the words, "This is my body... this is my blood," argued for a far more spiritual understanding of the whole chapter, and for the need for faith in those who celebrated the eucharist.

Rather surprisingly, in the bitter disputes which followed, hardly anyone seems to have challenged at all the basic assumed connection between John 6 and the eucharist. Even when commentators accepted, largely without question, that John's Gospel was exactly what it claims to be, an authentic record of the actual words of Jesus at various times in his ministry, the fact that the words of Jesus in the chapter were spoken months, if not a year or two, before the Last Supper, was not considered to be a problem. Jesus, it was claimed, was anticipating the Supper, and expanding on the meaning of his words there, beforehand. Modern opinion, which regards the fourth Gospel as the author's reflections on the ministry of Jesus set in the context of various incidents in it, has strengthened the eucharistic connection. John 6 is regarded as an obvious commentary on the meaning of the eucharist and should be understood accordingly.

Yet not only are Jesus' words in John 6 not set in the context of the Last Supper and therefore of the eucharist; a careful reading of them does not require a eucharistic interpretation at all. Jesus' words arise initially out of his complaint that the people are thronging him because he has just given them a good meal, and not because he can lead them to eternal life. "I am the bread of life," he says. "He who comes to me shall not hunger, and he who believes in me shall never thirst" (John 6:35). How could Jesus be saying more clearly that "eating him" involves coming to him, and "drinking him" consists of believing in him. That is what the people must do. They must come to him because he has come from the Father. They must believe in him because the Father has sent him. And as they enter into so close a relationship with him he will give them eternal life. Such language is the customary language of the fourth Gospel where Jesus is also portrayed as the living water which must be drunk, the light which must be followed, and the door which must be entered.

Now, to be sure, participating in the eucharist is one way, indeed a very important way, in which Christians can enjoy deep fellowship with Christ, and to that extent the words of John 6 can have a eucharistic connotation. But the eucharist is not the only way in which Christians can know their Lord. An ongoing acceptance of his claims in an alien and apathetic world; day by day trust in his presence and provision; natural, believing prayer as a child to his father; fellowship with others; active Christian service; in all these and other ways too, the Christian can know Christ and the power of his resurrection, sharing his sufferings, becoming like him in his death, that if possible he may attain the resurrection from the dead (Philippians 3:10,11). Had Christians in former times been more careful to set Christ's discourse on the bread of life in this wider context many unnecessary and bitter disputes need never have occurred.

d — "Do this in remembrance of me."

Fundamental to the annual Passover festival was the concept of memorial and remembrance. "This day shall be for you a memorial day," says Exodus 12:14, "and you shall keep it as a feast to the LORD; throughout your generations you shall observe it as an ordinance for ever." Again, in Deuteronomy: "You shall offer the passover sacrifice to the LORD your God . . . that all the days of your life you may remember the day when you came out of the land of Egypt" (Deuteronomy 16:2, 3). So when Jesus took bread at the Last Supper, gave thanks, broke it and said, "This is my body which is for you. Do this in remembrance of me," he was not only identifying himself as the new Passover lamb. He was also transferring the concept of memorial from the annual Passover feast to the new eucharistic meal he was instituting.

At first sight, Jesus' command could not appear to be more simple. Just as his disciples had offered the Passover sacrifice year by year so that "all the days of your life you may remember the day when you came out of Egypt," now they are to break bread that they might remember how Jesus, the Lamb of God, had brought them into a new relationship with God himself. It would seem to be as simple as that: "break bread that you may remember me." And that is exactly what, for the last four hundred years, the majority of Protestants have held that Jesus meant by his word. Jesus' actions at the Last Supper are simply to be repeated so that his followers might remember his work on their behalf.

However, fundamental to the work of Christ on the cross was the offering of a sacrifice to God. That was what Jesus did when he died. He offered himself to restore a lost humanity to God.

Now, if the eucharist is a symbol of the death of Christ, so vivid that it may be called by what it signifies, and if the death of Christ was a sacrifice, does it not follow that the celebration of the eucharist constitutes the offering of a sacrifice as well? This idea has indeed been integral to the development of eucharistic thought from the very beginning of the Christian church. It remains crucial to Orthodox and Catholic understanding to the present day. Since the Reformation, however, many Protestants have denied that the celebration of the eucharist constitutes the offering of a sacrifice, while others have only been willing to use sacrificial language with many reservations and in a very carefully controlled way. The nature of eucharistic sacrifice remains one of the sharpest points of difference between Catholics and Protestants at the present time. Nor are the issues involved unimportant; at their heart lies the essential nature of the Gospel itself.

Of recent years the battle over eucharistic sacrifice has been joined over the meaning of Jesus' words, "Do this in remembrance of me." Using their vastly increased knowledge of classical Hebrew and New Testament Greek which has become available to them, some modern scholars have suggested, for example, that the purpose of the Passover festival was not to remind the Israelites of what God had done, but to enable the Israelites to remind God of what he had done for them in the past with a plea that he act in a similarly decisive way again.[4]

If the purpose of the Passover sacrifice was to remind God, rather than men, of what he had done, does it not follow that the purpose of the eucharistic sacrifice will be similar? Support for the idea that the eucharist really does constitute the offering of a sacrifice is found in the assertion that the words, "Do this," should really be translated, "Offer this."[5] Support for the idea that in the eucharist God is to remember rather than the followers of Jesus is the assertion that "in remembrance of me", should read, "that God may remember me."[6] Perhaps those scholars who have suggested that the eucharist is intended to remind both God and men of what Jesus has done in his death on the cross have the most positive contribution to make to an otherwise inconclusive debate.[7]

Now there is a world of difference between a command to, "do this in remembrance of me," which means, "repeat this symbolic action so that you may never forget what I have done for you," and a command to, "offer this sacrifice that God may remember me and act again on your behalf." The implications of that difference are reflected in the widely differing ways in which Christians celebrate the eucharist. The cry is often heard that eucharistic worship, like all Christian worship, should be conducted in accordance with the teaching of the Word of God. But when Biblical scholars of integrity reach such widely different conclusions about the meaning of the Word of God, that only indicates how intractable is the problem. In such a situation the only Christian way forward must be the way of love, of mutual respect and of deep humility. It is hopefully in this spirit that this book is offered as a contribution to the current eucharistic debate.

e — "The new covenant in my blood."

Fundamental to the Jews' understanding of their relationship with God was the idea of covenant. God had chosen their ancestor Abraham for no other reason than that he loved him and had entered into a solemn, binding agreement with him to be his God and to make him the father of the Jewish nation (see Genesis 12 and 15). At Passover, and later at Sinai after the Israelites had escaped from Egypt, God renewed his covenant with Abraham's descendants and made them his people. He promised, for his part, to be their God, and required them, for their part, to keep his law. With Abraham, and with the Israelites, the covenants were ratified with animal sacrifices (see Genesis 15, Exodus 24).

Now the sad story of the Old Testament is the story of Israel's failure to keep its part of the covenant. Again and again, the nation broke God's laws and brought judgment on itself. Again and again, God renewed his covenant in times of national repentance and renewal and proved utterly faithful to his promises.

Not that the Israelites were entirely to blame for their failure. To some extent the covenant itself was to blame for its demands were too hard. Since God is perfect he required perfect obedience to his law, and that is impossible for anyone, let alone a whole nation. Even when obedience was forthcoming it was mostly in external things only and led to hypocritical self-righteousness in those who were apparently successful. What was needed was a covenant in which the requirements of God's law were not merely laid down, but a covenant which enabled the participants to obey as well.

To the establishment of this new covenant the prophets Jeremiah and Ezekiel looked forward. "Behold, the days are coming, says the LORD, when I will make a new covenant with the house of Israel and the house of Judah.... I will put my law within them, and I will write it upon their hearts; and I will be their God, and they shall be my people" (Jeremiah 31:31,33). "A new heart I will give you, and a new spirit I will put within you; and I will take out of your flesh the heart of stone and give you a heart of flesh. And I will put my spirit within you, and cause you to walk in my statutes and be careful to observe my ordinances" (Ezekiel 36:27, 28).

At the Last Supper, Jesus claimed that his death would be the sacrifice which would ratify this new covenant. So those who trusted him would be forgiven their sins and made into God's new people. Thus the eucharist is not simply an individual affair whereby the worshipper "makes his communion". In the eucharist the church worships and should be conscious of its calling as the body of Christ.

f — "As often as you drink it."

How often did Jesus intend his disciples to eat bread and drink wine, "in remembrance of me"? Every time they had a meal? That would have made the eucharist a private, family festival. Once a year, as in the annual Passover festival? In that case, most of the church has been far too enthusiastic in obeying Christ's command. Even the most radical of the Reformers who, as will be seen, underrated the eucharist in favour of the proclamation of the Word, advocated quarterly communions.

Towards the end of the Passover meal a cup of wine called, "the cup of blessing," was drunk. Paul makes it quite clear that it was over this cup that Christ said, "This cup is the new covenant in my blood" (see 1 Corinthians 10:16). Now, modern scholars have discovered that besides being drunk at the annual Passover festival, the cup of blessing was drunk weekly, at a communal festive meal at the start of the Sabbath. Significantly, according to Paul, it is only over the cup that Jesus says, "as often as you drink it"; over the bread he simply says, "do this". This has led some scholars to suggest that Jesus was prescribing a weekly meal when he instituted the eucharist.[8] Whether he was or not, the weekly Lord's Day was already well established in the pattern of Christian worship by the end of the first century (see Revelation 1:10), and eucharistic celebration was quite properly included in that worship (see Acts 20:7).

There seems little point in being dogmatic about this particular conclusion. Nonetheless, weekly eucharists have much to commend them from a purely practical point of view. It is possible to despise the eucharist by ignoring it and attending it only rarely. On the other hand, did Jesus really intend the daily eucharists so apparently necessary in some Catholic circles, both in the Church of Rome and in the Church of England? It must be very difficult to prevent the eucharist from becoming mere routine if one is attending or celebrating it so often. Weekly eucharists at least maintain a sense of proportion and balance and are sensible as a general rule.

g — "You proclaim the Lord's death."

After describing to the Corinthian Christians what happened on the night when Jesus was betrayed, Paul adds a sentence of comment and explanation. "For as often as you eat this bread and drink the cup," he says, "you proclaim the Lord's death until he comes" (1 Corinthians 11:26). That is what the eucharist is. It is a proclamation of the Lord's death. To whom then is the proclamation made?

Those who believe that the eucharistic celebration is a sacrificial offering intended to remind God of the death of his Son naturally assume that the proclamation is made to God. Those who believe that the eucharist is merely a memorial to remind men of the death of Christ see it equally naturally as a proclamation to men. Indeed, many would suggest that Paul's words contain more than a hint that verbal proclamation is an essential ingredient of a proper eucharistic celebration. Of themselves, the repetition of Christ's actions and words over the bread and the cup are not quite enough. The Word should be proclaimed as well, so that the people might receive additional instruction and encouragement in their Christian lives. At various times in history, the eucharist has been exalted and the Word neglected, and at other times the opposite has happened. What is needed is a balanced emphasis on both Word and eucharist at all times.

What did Paul mean by "the Lord's death"? — ask a silly question! Obviously, he meant Christ's last hours on the cross when his body was broken and his blood outpoured. But did he mean more? Was Christ's death all there was to his work of redemption? Were his earthly life, his resurrection and ascension, and continuing intercession in heaven not involved as well? Will not his coming again bring his work of redemption to completion?

Much modern scholarly opinion takes the view that the Christian churches of the West, dominated by the Church of Rome, became increasingly preoccupied with the death of Christ to the neglect of all other aspects of his work. This preoccupation was continued by Protestants at the time of the Reformation and is particularly seen in evangelical theology at the present time. In the Orthodox churches of the East, however, the emphasis is placed much more heavily on the resurrection, and the death of Christ is regarded, not as fundamental to his work, but as a necessary prelude to the events of Easter morning. Furthermore, it is suggested, that when Paul said, "You proclaim the Lord's death," he was using a kind of shorthand expression which in fact meant, "You proclaim the whole of the Lord's work, his death and his resurrection."

Certainly, the logic in this argument is attractive. Christ's death must never indeed be separated from the rest of his work on earth. Christians worship a living Lord who has left dramatic confirmation of his triumph over death and all the powers of darkness in the evidence of the empty tomb. On the other hand, Paul's frequent references to the blood of Christ and the cross of Christ indicate that his death was the most fundamental element in his work. If modern opinion is genuinely concerned with correcting an error of over-emphasis, that is fair enough. Any movement, however, which detracts from the importance of the death of Christ, should be treated with great caution lest, in correcting over-emphasis, it becomes guilty of under-emphasis itself. After all, it is broken bread, and poured-out wine which are consumed in the eucharist.

h — "Until he comes."

Should Christians look backwards or forwards when they celebrate the eucharist? When they were under pressure during the first three centuries of their existence they naturally looked forwards to the return of Christ and the conquest of his enemies. When the pressure relaxed and the danger of persecution passed, Christians started to look backwards and to dwell on the final events of Jesus' life.

Paul says that, in the eucharist, Christians should look backwards and forwards. They should look backwards to the cross, where their redemption was secured, and they should look forwards to Christ's coming again when the redemption which was won at Calvary will be brought to its final consummation. There is a glorious eschatalogical emphasis. Christ promised that he would drink the wine with his disciples in his kingdom. His experienced spiritual presence when he is remembered in the breaking of the bread anticipates his visible presence when he comes to complete and glorify his church.

> And thus that dark betrayal night
> With the last advent we unite.
> By one blest chain of loving rite,
>   Until he come.
>   (George Rawson)

THE LAST SUPPER

i — Participation in the Body and Blood of Christ

Besides describing the eucharist as a proclamation of the Lord's death until he comes, Paul also insists that it is a participation, or sharing, in the body and blood of Christ, binding many individual Christians together into one. "The cup of blessing which we bless," he writes, is it not a participation in the blood of Christ? The bread which we break, is it not a participation in the body of Christ? Because there is one bread, we who are many are one body, for we all partake of the one bread" (1 Corinthians 10:16,17).

For centuries Christians have debated whether or not anything happens to the bread and wine in the eucharist. Paul, however, is concerned, not with the effect of the eucharist on the elements, but on the people who are involved in it. He uses language as startlingly realistic as the author of the fourth Gospel does in John chapter 6. In the eucharist, Christians share in the body and blood of Christ. In the eucharist, they become one body. "Whoever, therefore, eats the bread or drinks the cup of the Lord in an unworthy manner will be guilty of profaning the body and blood of the Lord. Let a man examine himself, and so eat of the bread and drink of the cup. For any one who eats and drinks without discerning the body eats and drinks judgment upon himself. That is why many of you are weak and ill, and some have died" (1 Corinthians 11:27–30).

All of this is set in the context of the question: Should Christians eat meat that had been offered to idols? Although conceding that idols had no real existence, Paul nonetheless counselled against the practice on the grounds, "that what pagans sacrifice they offer to demons and not to God. I do not want you to be partners with demons. You cannot drink the cup of the Lord and the cup of demons. You cannot partake of the table of the Lord and the table of demons" (1 Corinthians 10:20, 21). Paul is thus quite convinced: eucharistic worship has an effect on the worshipper for good or ill.

Since the Reformation, Protestants have debated whether the eucharist is an ordinance or a sacrament. That is to say, should

Christians engage in eucharistic worship, simply because Christ commanded them to, with no particular benefits following on that worship beyond the natural effect that good will always follow from obedience, or should they engage in eucharistic worship because the eucharist is a means of grace bringing direct blessing as a result? For Paul, the eucharist brings direct blessing (or judgment) and therefore should be regarded as a sacrament and not merely an ordinance.

j — Eucharistic Worship in the First Century

How did the earliest Christians actually celebrate the eucharist? The question is important, for, as has been observed already, the cry is often heard that if only Christians worshipped according to the New Testament pattern, then all would be well; abuse, dispute and division would cease.

The trouble is, of course, that while the New Testament provides four descriptions of the institution of the Lord's Supper, it says very little about the way in which the followers of Jesus actually translated his command into practice. The first converts "devoted themselves... to the breaking of bread" (Acts 2:42), but the fact that they did this "in their homes" (Acts 2:46) while meeting in the temple for other worship has led many scholars to conclude that this is not a eucharistic reference. Later the Acts records a meeting for the breaking of bread on the first day of the week in the church at Troas (Acts 20:7), but the form of this meeting was quite clearly unusual since it included a long sermon by Paul "until midnight" (see Acts 20:7). The Gospels themselves, of course, were almost certainly written with the needs of the worshipping communities in mind, and the inclusion of the institution of the eucharist in them was done to regulate eucharistic celebrations. It thus follows that New Testament period eucharists included the repetition of the words of Jesus at the Last Supper, the eating of bread and the drinking of wine. But then, all Christian eucharists today include those elements, yet Christians still manage to fall out with each other about the vastly different ways in which those apparently simple things are to be done.

All this only leaves the church at Corinth. Paul says more about eucharistic faith and practice in 1 Corinthians than in all his other letters put together. But even here his material is not altogether helpful to twentieth-century Christians concerned with restoring, "the purity of New Testament worship." For in Corinth, the eucharist was being abused. It was being combined with a longer meal to which, apparently, everybody brought their own food. As a result, the wealthy members of the church were eating sumptuously, while the poor, including presumably the slaves, were going hungry (see 1 Corinthians 11:21). Not only so, the rich apparently were not willing to wait for the poor to arrive before starting the meal, and so the eucharist was not being celebrated by all the Christians together. None of this is very helpful in establishing a New Testament pattern of worship.

If the discussion is extended to cover the rest of the Corinthians' worship a pattern emerges of a free and easy gathering in which "each one has a hymn, a lesson, a revelation, a tongue, or an interpretation" (1 Corinthians 14:26). But Paul is not altogether happy with this state of affairs either and counsels that "all things should be done decently and in order" (1 Corinthians 14:40).

Nor does it necessarily follow that the "charismatic" style of worship practised in Corinth was typical of Christian worship in general during the first century. It may have been, but there is no definite evidence either way. What is significant is that when details of actual eucharistic celebrations begin to emerge from various churches in the second and third centuries they all have one remarkable feature in common: they are all modelled on the form of the Jewish synagogue services of the first century with the specific eucharistic material added on. Now what in the world could have caused Christian Gentile congregations in the second and third centuries to be following Jewish forms of services from the first century unless those forms of service had been handed down during the previous one or two hundred years? So perhaps Christian worship in the first century was not as spontaneous as some have commonly supposed. Perhaps there were set forms of services after all, and even if, perhaps, those services were not always followed word for word, the pattern was there and the content was there.

Another factor which the eucharistic services of the second and third centuries have in common is this: the churches from which they originated all believed that the liturgies (that is, the forms of services) had been handed down from the apostles themselves. This is still true of the Orthodox churches of the east. They are absolutely convinced that their eucharistic celebrations originated with the apostles and therefore their form should be preserved at all costs.

In fact, it is impossible to know precisely how Christians in the first century celebrated the eucharist. In all probability there was wide diversity of practice. Spontaneous material and liturgical form probably co-existed side by side. More significantly, the various forms of worship in the developing Christian churches, would have reflected the social composition of the congregations and the wider structure of society at large. For since worship is a corporate activity it must satisfy the social and psychological needs of the worshippers. And since society changes, worship must change too, or wither and die.

For this reason, it is impossible to have worship without tradition. The quest for the New Testament pattern of worship is a chimera. Even if it were found it would be totally irrelevant to the needs of the present day. Thus, every attempt to rediscover and recreate worship according to the New Testament has only succeeded in creating a new tradition which, when it has become impervious to change, has become arid and dead.

Of course there are aspects of New Testament worship which are timeless; breaking bread, drinking the cup, remembering the Lord in his death. But the application of those aspects will vary from place to place, from country to country, and from one generation to another. If at any time practices are adopted and beliefs encouraged which are contrary to the fundamental truths of the New Testament revelation, then, unless those mistakes are corrected, that congregation, or denomination, or whatever, will come to stand outside the authentic Christian tradition. But within that tradition there is room for variety, innovation and change. That is one reason why there are so many different expressions of the tradition within the total Body of Christ, the church.

CHAPTER ONE NOTES

1 – See Matthew 26:17; Mark 14:12; Luke 22:7, 8.
   Joachim Jeremias, *The Eucharistic Words of Jesus*, is a detailed argument in favour of the accuracy of these verses.
2 – Dom Gregory Dix bases the whole of his monumental work on the eucharist, *The Shape of the Liturgy*, on this assertion.
3 – In the Revised Standard Version of the Bible this detail, in Luke's Gospel, is relegated to a footnote. In *The Eucharistic Words of Jesus*, Jeremias has argued that this footnote is an integral part of the Gospel, and should be treated accordingly.
4 – See, e.g., Paul Tihon, *Theology of the Eucharistic Prayer*, in ed. Lancelot Sheppard, *The New Liturgy*, pp. 178, 179, and Joachim Jeremias, *The Eucharistic Words of Jesus*, p. 249.
   For a refutation of this view see, e.g., J. A. Motyer, *Priestly Sacrifice in the Old Testament*, in ed. J. I. Packer, *Eucharistic Sacrifice*, pp. 31–36.
5 – For a useful summary of scholars reaching this conclusion see David Gregg, *Anamnesis in the Eucharist*, p. 14, footnote 5.
   For a refutation of this position see Thomas Hewitt, *The Development of Eucharistic Doctrine up to the English Reformation*, in ed. J. I. Packer, *Eucharistic Sacrifice*, pp. 91–93.
6 – See, Joachim Jeremias, *The Eucharistic Words of Jesus*, pp. 237–255, and Dom Gregory Dix, *The Shape of the Liturgy*, p. 243.
   For a refutation of this view see D. M. Baillie, *The Theology of the Sacraments*, p. 111 and Thomas Hewitt, *The Development of Eucharistic Doctrine up to the English Reformation*, in ed. J. I. Packer, *Eucharistic Sacrifice*, pp. 93, 94.
7 – See David Gregg, *Anamnesis in the Eucharist*, p. 24.
8 – For a more academic presentation of this evidence see David Gregg, *Anamnesis in the Eucharist*, p. 16.

CHAPTER 2 — THE WORK OF CHRIST

The previous chapter demonstrated how the eucharist was instituted as a vivid symbol of the work of Christ for men's salvation. In particular, passing reference was made to the fact that, in his death, Christ offered himself as a sacrifice to atone for human sin. The possible implications of this for a proper understanding of the eucharist were outlined, and areas of disagreement were set out. Yet so important is this aspect of Christ's work, and so crucial is a proper understanding of the nature of eucharistic sacrifice in the present climate of opinion, that the subject must be treated in more detail.

a — Sacrifice in the Old Testament

Scholars, have spilled large amounts of ink speculating on the origins of animal sacrifice in human history. In its description of the different sacrifices offered by Cain and Abel (Genesis 4:3–5), and in its account of how the LORD God clothed Adam and his wife in garments of skins when he expelled them from the Garden of Eden (Genesis 3:21), the Bible places the origin of sacrifice at the very dawn of human history itself.

Besides the origin of sacrifice, scholars have also speculated on the meaning of sacrifice, and, as in other areas of Biblical interpretation have drawn widely different conclusions. The key verse is held to be Leviticus 17:11: "for the life of the flesh is in the blood; and I have given it for you upon the altar to make atonement for your souls; for it is the blood that makes atonement, by reasons of the life." From this passage, some scholars have concluded that in killing an animal as a sacrifice the worshipper is releasing its life and offering it to God.[1] Other scholars, however, have insisted that in sacrifice, the animal is dying a substitutionary death instead of the worshipper, and that what is important therefore is life violently taken rather than the continued presence of life for some new purpose.[2]

This apparently abstruse debate has profound implications for a proper understanding of the sacrificial death of Christ and for the nature of the eucharistic sacrifice. For if, in his death, Jesus was offering his life to God, then his self-offering can be regarded as in some sense continuing, and the idea can be developed that in the eucharist, Christ, through his body which is the church, is somehow re-presenting the sacrifice of his life to the Father. If, on the other hand, Christ's death was a substitutionary death for sinners deserving death under the just judgment of God, then Christ's sacrificial offering is complete, and can no more be re-presented in the eucharist than it can be regarded as continuing in heaven.

The former view of the eucharist, the re-presentation view, is held by many modern Catholic thinkers, particularly in the Church of England. The latter view, the substitutionary view, is now largely the preserve of evangelical thinkers, who often see themselves as upholding the true principles of the Protestant Reformation.

Because sacrifices, in the Old Testament, made atonement for sin, they kept the whole Israelite nation and individuals within it in touch with God. Consequently, in the minds of some, they came to assume overwhelming importance. The highest service men could give to God consisted in the offering of sacrifices. Besides that, little else mattered. But in the Old Testament also, are the beginnings of a reaction against such a view, early demands that other forms of service may be more important. Indeed, sacrifices themselves may not be as pleasing to God as had sometimes been imagined; under certain circumstances they may be positively hateful to him. Thus, for instance, after the battle of Amalek when Saul spared the enemy's cattle to sacrifice them, instead of destroying them in accordance with God's command, Samuel asked:

> Has the LORD as great delight in burnt offerings and sacrifices,
>   as in obeying the voice of the LORD?
> Behold, to obey is better than sacrifice,
>   and to hearken than the fat of rams.
>
> (1 Samuel 15:22)

In similar vein in the penitential Psalm 51 the writer cries:

> For thou hast no delight in sacrifice;
> > were I to give a burnt offering, thou wouldst not be pleased.
> The sacrifice acceptable to God is a broken spirit;
> > a broken and contrite heart, O God, thou wilt not despise.
>
> (vv. 16, 17)

And in particularly strident tones the prophet Isaiah condemns the whole sacrificial system because the Israelites are offering sacrifices for atonement with no real repentance in their hearts:

> What to me is the multitude of your sacrifices?
> > says the LORD,
> I have had enough of burnt offerings of rams
> > and the fat of fed beasts;
> I do not delight in the blood of bulls,
> > or of lambs, or of he-goats . . .
>
> Your new moons and your appointed feasts
> > my soul hates;
> they have become a burden to me,
> > I am weary of bearing them . . .
>
> Wash yourselves; make yourselves clean;
> > remove the evil of your doings
> > from before my eyes;
> cease to do evil,
> > learn to do good;
> seek justice,
> > correct oppression;
> defend the fatherless,
> > plead for the widow.
>
> (Isaiah 1:11, 14, 16, 17)

Thus, obedience, penitence and repentance please God more than sacrifices.

In Psalm 50 is also the beginning of another development with regard to sacrifices. Not only do sacrifices not please God because they are not offered in the right frame of mind by the worshipper. Because God is Creator and Lord of the universe, man can offer nothing to him because what man has belongs to God already, and the only sacrifice that man can therefore bring is the sacrifice of thanksgiving for God's bountiful provision for his needs:

> Listen, my people, and I will speak;
> I will bear witness against you, O Israel:
> I am God, your God,
> shall I not find fault with your sacrifices,
> though your offerings are before me always?
> I need take no young bull from your house,
> > no he-goat from your folds;
> for all the beasts of the forest are mine
> > and the cattle in thousands on my hills.
> I know every bird on those hills,
> the teeming life of the fields is my care.
> If I were hungry, I would not tell you,
> for the world and all that is in it are mine.
> > Shall I eat the flesh of your bulls
> > or drink the blood of he-goats?
> Offer to God the sacrifice of thanksgiving
> and pay your vows to the Most High.
> > If you call upon me in time of trouble,
> > I will come to your rescue, and you shall honour me.
>
> (verses 7–15 NEB)

This idea, that God can be offered nothing because all is his already is taken up in the New Testament. Speaking to the Athenians on the Areopagus Paul declared, "The God who made the world and everything in it, being Lord of heaven and earth, does not live in shrines made by man, nor is he served by human hands, as though he needed anything, since he himself gives to all men life and breath and everything" (Acts 17:24, 25).

The point has important implications for the eucharist, for a fundamental part of a Catholic eucharist is the offertory, when the bread and wine, along with the people's monetary gifts are solemnly brought in procession to the altar or holy table and offered to God. They represent the fruits of the earth, and are offered in thanksgiving for its creation and in anticipation of its final redemption. As will shortly be seen, the offertory has a long and honoured pedigree, having been practised in the church from the very earliest times. It undoubtedly reflects the Jewish origins of the eucharist in the Passover celebration and the association of first fruits with that festival.

The question is, is it right? For at the Reformation the offertory was generally abandoned by the new Protestant churches on the basis of Psalm 50 and Acts 17, and the teaching of the Bible that salvation is all of grace and can only be gratefully received by sinful man. Rather than carried in procession the bread and wine came to be placed on the table before the celebration, and only the monetary gifts of the people continued to be brought forward and received with prayer.

The issue continues to divide Catholics and Protestants. Protestants suspect that the offertory shows that for Catholics the eucharist is a sacrifice intended to have an effect on God. They claim that the eucharist can be no more than a sacrifice of praise and thanksgiving for all God's mercies. However ancient the offertory might be, it should be abandoned as a Jewish hangover along with all the other demands of the ceremonial law. For Catholics the antiquity of the offertory is its own justification, for is not the church the body of Christ, indwelt by the Spirit of Christ? How could the earliest Christians have made such a fundamental mistake in the development of their eucharistic faith and practice?

b — The Sacrifice of Christ

The writers of the New Testament, as has been seen, do not hesitate to describe the work of Christ in sacrificial terms. Thus, both

Matthew and Mark recount how Jesus himself said he had come, "not to be served but to serve, and to give his life as a ransom for many" (Matthew 20:28; Mark 10:45). The apostle Paul tells the Corinthians how "Christ, our paschal lamb, has been sacrificed" (1 Corinthians 5:7), and the Ephesians how "Christ loved us and gave himself up for us, a fragrant offering and sacrifice to God" (5:2). The First Letter of Peter describes how its readers "were ransomed from the futile ways inherited from your fathers ... with the precious blood of Christ, like that of a lamb without blemish or spot" (1:18, 19). This description of Christ as a lamb is frequently employed in the Gospel and Revelation of John. There, Jesus is "the Lamb of God, who takes away the sin of the world" (John 1:29), while in heaven he appears as "a Lamb standing, as though it had been slain" (Revelation 5:6).

It is however, principally in the Letter to the Hebrews that the implications of the sacrificial work of Christ are most fully developed. A profound grasp of the author's teaching is essential to a proper understanding of the nature of the eucharistic sacrifice. The constant theme of the writer to the Hebrews is that what God has done in Christ is better than all he ever did through Moses and the prophets. Jesus was better than angels (chapters 1, 2), better than Moses (chapter 3), better than Aaron (chapter 7) and the sacrifice he offered was better than all the Jewish sacrifices put together because it has secured "an eternal redemption" (9:12). Indeed, the new covenant which God has made with man in Christ has made the old one obsolete. "And what is becoming obsolete and growing old is ready to vanish away" (8:13).

But the writer to the Hebrews is concerned not only with Christ's sacrifice. He also, more than any other New Testament author, develops the theme of his priesthood. Any sacrificial system needs priests who stand between the worshippers and God and offer the sacrifices on their behalf. Among the Israelites the priests were drawn from the sons of Aaron, and the sacrifices they offered were the animals and the cereals brought by the people. Jesus, however, combined in himself the work of priest and sacrifice. Because he lived a spotless life he became a perfect priest offering a perfect sacrifice and because his sacrifice was perfect it was offered once and can never be repeated (7:26–28).

This once-for-all nature of Christ's sacrifice is stressed again and again in the Letter to the Hebrews, so crucial is it to its author's understanding of the work of Christ. "He has no need like those high priests, to offer sacrifices daily, first for his own sins and then for those of the people; he did this *once for all* when he offered up himself" (7:27). "When Christ appeared as a high priest of the good things that have come . . . he entered *once for all* into the Holy Place, not through the blood of goats and calves but through his own blood, thus securing an eternal redemption" (9:12 margin). "He has appeared *once for all* at the end of the age to put away sin by the sacrifice of himself. And just as it is appointed for men to die once, and after that comes judgment, so Christ, *having been offered once* to bear the sins of many, will appear a second time, not to deal with sin but to save those who are eagerly waiting for him" (9:26–28). "When Christ had offered *for all time* a single sacrifice for sins, he sat down at the right hand of God, then to wait until his enemies should be made a stool for his feet. For by *a single offering* he has perfected *for all time* those who are sanctified" (10:12–14). As a result sins and misdeeds are remembered no more and "where there is forgiveness of these, there is no longer any offering for sin" (10:17, 18).

"It is finished" (John 19:30), cried Christ from the cross as he completed the sacrificial offering of himself. The point is vital in any discussion of eucharistic theology, for there have always been those who deliberately or unwittingly have attempted to compromise this aspect of his work. During the Middle Ages the eucharist came to be thought of as a repetition of the sacrifice of Christ, wherein Christ was re-offered again and again to atone for the sins of the worshippers. Attendance at the eucharist became the means of forgiveness, the sacrifice of the mass became more important than the sacrifice of Christ himself (at least in popular thinking) and the joyful sense of assurance and pardon so characteristic of New Testament Christianity was lost.

c — Sacrificial Christian Worship

Does this then imply that the idea of sacrifice should never intrude into Christian worship? There is certainly a sense in which this is so. Christian worship is unique in this respect. Unlike every other religion it points back triumphantly to what has already been accomplished rather than forwards wistfully to what may perhaps be achieved. There is nothing the Christian can do, either individually, or in the fellowship of the church, to put himself right with God, for Christ in his death has done all that is necessary. Any attempt to copy or repeat or add to what Christ has already done can only detract from it or cast doubts on its completeness and perfection.

> Nothing in my hand I bring
> Simply to thy cross I cling
> All for sin could not atone
> Thou must save and thou alone

is the language of the Christian.

Thus Christian worship can never be "sacrificial", if by that is meant inducing God to act on the Christian's behalf by making the Christian acceptable to God. God himself has already acted in Christ, decisively and finally. Christian worship is the thankful acceptance of and response to that fact.

Nevertheless the New Testament does in fact use sacrificial language to describe Christian worship and service. The very writer to the Hebrews who stresses the unrepeatable character of Christ's sacrificial work urges his readers to "offer up a sacrifice of praise to God" (Hebrews 13:15). A glance at a Bible Concordance will reveal how often, and in what senses, Christian writers employ sacrificial language.

First of all worship is a sacrifice. Peter speaks of the Christian community as "a spiritual house, a holy priesthood, to offer spiritual sacrifices acceptable to God through Jesus Christ" (1 Peter 2:5). The expression "spiritual sacrifices" of course excludes any thought of a visible offering of material things. It is the "worship in spirit and in truth" of which Jesus spoke, and which depends on no particular geographical location (John 4:21–24). Vocal worship; the use of words and music, is specified by the writer to the Hebrews. "Through Christ let us continually offer up a *sacrifice* of praise to God, that is *the fruit of lips* that acknowledge his name" (Hebrews 13:15). In this kind of thinking the word "sacrifice" has the double connotation of the trouble and care which the worshipper gives, and the sense that all that he can offer is his response to the once-for-all sacrifice of Christ.

This is equally emphasised in the second use of sacrificial language employed in the New Testament — that of the church in mission. This is a striking emphasis not always sufficiently noticed. The apostle Paul devoted his life to evangelism, "enduring suffering (to) do the work of an evangelist. *For* I am already on the point of being sacrificed" (2 Timothy 4:5, 6). He saw his whole ministry in proclaiming the Gospel as a kind of spiritual liturgy, "Serving with my spirit in the Gospel of God's Son" (Romans 1:9). In the thrilling results of his preaching — a multitude of Gentile converts brought to God — he saw the vindication of his "*priestly service* of the Gospel of God, so that the *offering* of the Gentiles may be acceptable" (Romans 15:16).

Paul is not alone in this concept. Peter describes the church as the people who have been called out of pagan darkness into the glorious light of the Gospel so that they may be "a royal priesthood — declaring the wonderful deeds of him who called you" (1 Peter 2:9). It is a challenging thought: evangelism, involving all of God's people, is the sacrificial offering to God of earnest endeavour, consistent living and direct proclamation, that claims the attention of those still in darkness, not to some animal sacrifice or liturgical ceremony, but to the Saviour of the world. " 'Tis all my business here below, to cry: Behold the Lamb!" It is a curious and suggestive fact that the Latin word *missa* (Mass) is a corruption of *missio* (to send out) and referred originally to the final act of worship when the faithful were dismissed and sent out to bear witness — "Go forth into the world".

The third use of sacrificial language is even more striking. It describes the attitude to *finance* displayed by Christians. The apostle Paul was sent a financial gift by the recently-formed church at Philippi. Its purpose was to encourage him in his further evangelistic labours, but he saw it with deep emotion as "a fragrant *offering*, a *sacrifice* acceptable and pleasing to God" (Philippians 4:18). The writer to the Hebrews reflects something of the cheerful sharing of goods and mutual support so characteristic of the early church, and so often repeated in times of renewal and revival. "Do not neglect to do good and to share what you have, for such *sacrifices* are pleasing to God", he says (Hebrews 13:16). The blunt and down-to-earth writer James defines true cultic religion as the practical meeting of the needs of orphans and widows, thus reflecting the repeated theme of the Old Testament prophets. It may well be that these Christian writers, in using sacrificial language in this way are echoing the warning of Christ and his apostles that material possessions can easily become "gods", and that covetousness is a form of idolatry.

Finally, there are references to sacrifice in the right use of the Christian's body. In view of the amazing grace of God expressed in his saving Gospel, Christians are urged to yield their bodies "as a living *sacrifice*, holy and acceptable to God, which is your spiritual *worship*" (Romans 12:1). In Paul's own case he was prepared to face the likelihood of the martyrdom of his body, and this too he saw as a sacrifice and libation. "Even if I am to be poured out as a libation upon the sacrificial offering of your faith — " (Philippians 2:17) "I am already on the point of being sacrificed (2 Timothy 4:6).

To summarise then, the language of sacrifice is used in the New Testament in a wider context than that of sin and its atonement. As an atoning sacrifice, the death of Christ is unique and unrepeatable. But for those who come by faith into the benefits that flow from it, the whole of Christian living, service and worship is sacrificial and is offered as a response to that one supreme sacrifice of Christ. As long as the distinction between the two types of sacrifice is understood and maintained, there is no harm in using such language.

The bearing of all this on the eucharist should be obvious. Attempts were outlined in the previous chapter to interpret the eucharistic words of Jesus in a sacrificial way and from them, to conclude, that the eucharist is in some way intended to repeat or continue or re-present the sacrificial work of Christ before the throne of God in heaven. Dissatisfaction with those attempts was also outlined. When the specific eucharistic material of the New Testament is compared with the conclusions of the writer to the Hebrews any sacrificial description of the eucharist must be treated with the greatest of caution. Christ is not engaged in re-presenting his sacrificial work before the Father in heaven and the eucharist cannot therefore reflect such a re-presentation. In that sense the eucharist cannot be a sacrifice.

Nevertheless, Christians are urged to pray in the name of Jesus. On the basis of what Jesus has done, and of their standing in him, they are commanded to present themselves and their petitions to God. What is the eucharist, with its graphic reminder of the work of Christ, with its re-enactment of the words and actions of Christ at the Last Supper, but a most eloquent prayer "in the name of Jesus". Thus it calls forth a sacrifice of praise and thanksgiving from those who celebrate it. Equally it offers a continual challenge to its participants to present their bodies as a living sacrifice to God, which is their spiritual worship.

New Testament writers are not afraid to describe the eucharist in sacrificial terms. Within a eucharistic context Paul reminds the Corinthians that those who eat the sacrifices are partners in the altar, and argues therefrom, "You cannot drink the cup of the Lord and the cup of demons. You cannot partake of the table of the Lord and the table of demons" (see 1 Corinthians 10:14–22). In similar vein the writer to the Hebrews declares, "We have an altar from which those who serve the tent have no right to eat" (13:10). What can he mean but the eucharistic table?

Of course the eucharist is a sacrifice, as all Christian worship is a sacrifice. It is a sacrifice because it is the symbol of a sacrifice, and, as has been shown, it is perfectly permissible to call the symbol by the thing it signifies. But unlike the sacrifice of Christ himself, the eucharist is not an atoning nor an expiatory sacrifice. Sadly the Christian church has not always remained conscious of this subtle yet important difference, and in parts of the church there is great uncertainty at the present time. As a result the Supper that should unite Christians in their worship of the crucified and risen Lord continues to divide them.

d — The Presence of Christ

The author of Matthew's Gospel records Jesus as ending his earthly ministry with the words, "lo, I am with you always, to the close of the age" (28:20). Unlike the followers of other religions Christians not only look back to the teaching and example of their Founder, but also insist, that by virtue of his resurrection and the gift of his Spirit, he is with them now, as really as he was present with his disciples in Palestine two thousand years ago. How is Christ thus present? Three answers, generally, have been given to the question.

In the first place Christ is present with his people in the Holy Spirit. "It is to your advantage that I go away," said Jesus just before his passion, "for if I do not go away, the Counsellor will not come to you; but if I go, I will send him to you" (John 16:7). Through the Holy Spirit Christ comforts, guides and strengthens his people and makes them aware of his presence and reality. From time to time the church has lost the consciousness of Christ's presence in the Holy Spirit, and from time to time it has regained this consciousness in movements of spiritual renewal. Often regarded initially with suspicion these movements have later been recognised as having restored the sense of Christ's living presence in times of spiritual decline. Montanism, in the fourth century, is often regarded as the first example of such a movement. The charismatic movement is its contemporary manifestation.

Secondly, Christ is present when his people gather for worship and prayer. "Where two or three are gathered in my name," said Jesus, "there am I in the midst of them" (Matthew 18:20). Christianity is a corporate and not an individualistic faith. From the beginning Christians have met together for teaching, sharing and worship and have been encouraged to continue doing so when their enthusiasm has waned (see Hebrews 10:25). Christians are variously described as stones in a building (1 Peter 2:4, 5), branches in a tree (Romans 11:17–24) and members of a living body (1 Corinthians 12:12–31), all of which metaphors emphasise the corporate nature of their commitment. Thus, it is in their corporate activity together that Christians most vividly experience the presence of Christ.

Thirdly, because the eucharist is the central act of Christian worship Christ is present in a special way when it is celebrated. The exact nature of this special or Real Presence has been variously defined down the centuries. Because Jesus identified the eucharistic elements with his body and blood, his presence has often been centred in the bread and wine: in the eucharist the bread and wine become the body and blood of Christ, so that those who eat and drink feed on Christ as commanded in John 6. In the Catholic and Orthodox traditions the bread and wine are actually changed, *ex opere operato*, that is, automatically, as they are consecrated during the eucharist. In the Western church the change is effected by the repetition of the words of Jesus, "This is my body . . . this is my blood." In the Eastern church the change is effected by the Holy Spirit at a point in the liturgy called the *epiclesis* when the celebrant prays that by the power of the Spirit the gifts of bread and wine may be changed into the body and blood of Christ. Both traditions also demand a body of consecrated priests to preside at the eucharist, organised under bishops who claim to be able to trace their descent from the New Testament apostles themselves.

Among Protestants there is great variety in understanding of the Real Presence. Some, like Lutherans and Catholic Anglicans, are scarcely distinguishable from Western, or Roman, Catholics. Descendants of Calvin are conscious of the activity of the Holy Spirit in the eucharist although they reject the idea of an actual change in the elements. Others locate the Presence, not in any moment of consecration, but in the act of communion, when the bread and wine are received by the faithful. Still others reject any idea of change in the elements altogether, regarding Christ as being present only by faith in the hearts of the worshippers. Most Protestants restrict the celebration of the eucharist to a body of ordained ministers. Some, in theory at least, allow any of their number to celebrate, although in practice those who do is usually rather limited. How these classic positions developed and how they are all being re-examined and restated at the present time will occupy the remaining chapters of this book.

CHAPTER TWO NOTES

1 – See, e.g., Vincent Taylor, *Jesus and His Sacrifice*, pp. 54, 55.
2 – See, e.g., Leon Morris, *The Apostolic Preaching of the Cross*, p. 117.

CHAPTER 3 — TRIBULATION AND TRIUMPH

The first six hundred years of the Christian era marked the first main period in the Church's history. From a tiny group of Jews in Palestine, Christians not only grew in numbers to encompass the entire Roman Empire and beyond; they also defied the might of the Roman state for two and a half centuries and emerged to become the ascendant moral, social and political force in European society, a position they have held at least until very recent times. During this period also, Christian doctrine was defined and Christian worship, particularly eucharistic worship, reached the form and structure it has largely retained in the Catholic tradition of the church. The origin of most of the issues which today divide Christians in their interpretation of the eucharist can thus be traced back to this earliest period.

a — The Early Fathers

One of the first tasks of the church was to define its relationship to the Jewish faith. Christians were in a curious position. They proclaimed the God of the Jews and used the Jewish scriptures, whilst at the same time holding to a concept of salvation, a belief in the Messiah, and a way of life, utterly unacceptable to the average Jew. Their explanation of this anomaly was based on the teaching of Christ and its development by the apostolic writers. Not only was Jesus the long-promised Messiah, but by his death and resurrection he had fulfilled the promises and exhausted the demands of the Law. Jewish sacrifices were no longer necessary or valid; Jesus had superseded them by his death on the cross.

This meant a radical break with the type of worship which had been so familiar in the Temple. Worship could no longer find its climax in blood sacrifices. Its climax came instead in the eucharist, the remembrance of the sacrifice of Christ at Calvary. From the earliest days Christians quoted the prophecy of Malachi 1:11 as finding its fulfilment in the eucharist: "For from the rising of the sun to its setting, my name is great among the nations, and in every place incense is offered in my name, and a pure offering; for my name is great among the nations, says the LORD of hosts." The New Testament nowhere equates the "pure offering" of this prophecy with the eucharist and it is questionable if this is a fair interpretation of the passage, but to the early Christians, concerned to establish the superiority of their faith over Judaism the interpretation was self-evident; the eucharist was the Christian sacrifice.

One of the earliest Christians to write about the eucharist outside the pages of the New Testament was probably the author of the *Didache*. Modern scholars have differed widely over the date of this manual of Christian teaching, placing it anywhere and everywhere between the middle of the first century and the end of the second. That it does reflect a very early period in the development of the eucharist is evident from the way in which it appears to describe an *agape* or love-feast taking place at the same time as the eucharist proper. The issue is complex. Suffice to say the author prescribes a weekly celebration "on the Lord's day of the Lord . . . having first confessed your transgression, that your sacrifice may be pure. But let none who has a quarrel with his companion join with you until they have been reconciled, that your sacrifice may not be defiled. For this is that which was spoken by the Lord, 'In every place and at every time offer me a pure sacrifice; for I am a great king, says the Lord, and my name is wonderful among the nations.'"[1]

The main motif of the Didachean eucharist/agape is thanksgiving, thanksgiving over the cup "for the holy vine of your child David, which you made known to us through your child Jesus,"[2] thanksgiving over the bread, "to you, our Father, for the life and knowledge which you made known to us through your child Jesus,"[3] and a longer thanksgiving to the Father "after you have had your fill . . . for your holy name which you have enshrined in our hearts, and for the knowledge and faith and immortality which you made known to us through your child Jesus . . . You, Lord Almighty, created all things for the sake of your name and gave food and drink to men for their enjoyment, that they might give you thanks; but to us you have granted spiritual food and drink for eternal life through your child Jesus. Above all we give you thanks because you are mighty; glory to you for evermore. Amen."[4] Thus, in so far as the eucharist is a sacrifice it is a thank-offering and no more. In no sense is it a sacrifice in the older Jewish sense of an offering to appease or propitiate an angry god. In the sacrificial climate of the first and second centuries it was essential for the Christian church to have a sacrifice if it was to have any religious validity in the eyes of its members and potential converts. But the *Didache* makes it quite clear that the eucharist/agape was a sacrifice of quite a different order from those obtaining in Judaism or the pagan religions.

Thanksgiving is also the main element in the eucharist for Justin Martyr whose writings can confidently be dated around the middle of the second century. Justin was born in Syria, converted to Christianity about AD 130, lived for a time in Ephesus where he wrote his *Dialogue with Trypho* (a Jew), and later went to Rome. There he wrote his *Apologies* (or defences) for Christianity before being put to death for his faith in AD 165, hence his title Martyr. In the *Dialogue* he says "the bread of the eucharist" was "handed down to us . . . so that we might give thanks to God, both for creating the world with all things that are in it for the sake of man, and for freeing us from the evil in which we were born, and for accomplishing a complete destruction of the principalities and powers through his Son who suffered according to his will."[5] Equally with the Didache, the eucharist for Justin is a sacrifice offered in fulfilment of Malachi 1:11.[6] But "prayers and thanksgivings made by worthy men are the only sacrifices that are perfect and well-pleasing to God."[7] This equation of sacrifice with thanksgiving is the constant theme of all early writers on the eucharist. Thus Clement, bishop of Alexandria, in Egypt at the end of the second century and the beginning of the third wrote, "rightly we do not offer God, who has need of nothing who however has given men everything, an (external) gift; on the contrary, we glorify Him who dedicated Himself to us, by dedicating ourselves to Him."[8] And Origen, bishop of Caesarea later in the third century said, "we are not people with ungrateful hearts; it is true we do not sacrifice . . . to such beings who . . . are our enemies; but to God who has bestowed upon us an abundance of benefits . . . we fear being ungrateful. The sign of this gratitude towards God is the bread called Eucharist."[9] This early insistence on thanksgiving in the context of the eucharistic sacrifice needs to be remembered when later controversies arise and when the eucharistic sacrifice has come to be regarded in very different terms.

However, if the superiority of Christianity over Judaism was the main concern of the writer of the *Didache* a more subtle and dangerous threat to the truth of the Gospel was beginning to afflict the church by the time of Justin's *Apologies* and martyrdom. This threat was the hydra-headed system of Gnosticism. Traditionally founded by Simon Magus of Acts chapter 8 after his rejection by the apostle Peter, the Gnostics troubled the church for a hundred and fifty years at least. Orthodox leaders were forced into new definitions of their faith, in their attempts to combat the Gnostic influence.

Gnosticism was the expression of a climate of opinion rather than a clearly-defined movement. Its "christian" versions sprang from the enthusiastic but misguided efforts of some in the church to adjust the Christian message to prevailing fashions of thought, and thus make it more acceptable. A mixture of Greek and Oriental thinking led to presuppositions which seem odd or even grotesque to the modern mind, but which were as much taken for granted in the second century as democracy or evolution are in the twentieth. It was a fashion that regarded "matter" as intrinsically evil, and "spirit" as intrinsically good. The body (being material) was assumed to be the root of evil, while virtue was attained by the pursuit of "knowledge" (*gnosis*), the more secret and esoteric and exclusive the knowledge, the better.

It was fatally easy for misguided enthusiasts to clothe Christian thinking in this kind of language in order to preach an up-dated "Gospel" for contemporary man. The "god of the Old Testament" (who created the material world, and was thereby contaminated) was set over against the Father of the New Testament (who was supremely "spiritual"). A real incarnation was, of course, unthinkable (how could a holy God take flesh?), so Jesus was radically re-interpreted. Either he was a halfway figure between spirit and matter (one of the angelic-type "emanations" conceived as evolving in descending order from God, each a little less spiritual, a little more material), or he was an expression of God which only appeared to be human and only seemed to suffer. Against the early hints of the first view, Paul warns the Colossians, Christ "is the image of the invisible God, . . . in him all things were created, . . . in him all the fullness of God was pleased to dwell. . . . Let no one disqualify you, insisting on . . . worship of angels . . ." (Colossians 1:15, 16, 19; 2:18). Against the beginnings of the second view John writes his condemnation: "we have seen with our eyes, . . . and touched with our hands, . . . the word of life . . . every spirit which confesses that Jesus Christ has come in the flesh is of God" (1 John 1:1; 4:2).

The majority of Christian leaders recognised Gnosticism as utterly destructive of Christian teaching. It denied the creation, the incarnation, the atonement, the resurrection of Christ and the redemption of the body. Further developments of it into the area of ethics led either to extreme asceticism or to extreme permissiveness. It was a classic example of the danger of accommodating the Gospel to the passing climate of opinion. Opinions change, and the presuppositions of one age become the curiosities of the next. If Christianity had really thrown in its lot with Gnosticism, it would not have survived the third century. Men like Justin, Irenaeus and Tertullian fought it to a standstill and preserved the Gospel for succeeding generations.

In the fight against Gnosticism, however, Christian truth was inevitably redefined. For example, the regular Gnostic assertion that it possessed secret revelations and gospel narratives led to the collecting and defining of the New Testament canon. The Gnostic claim to inherit the true teaching of Jesus was answered by the idea of "apostolic succession". Here are the records of our church leaders, going back to each church's foundation by an apostle, the Christian argument ran. The doctrine has remained the same. Show us at what stage we are supposed to have departed from the tradition of Jesus!

Most of all, the orthodox leadership contended for the true incarnation of Christ. Jesus really had come in the flesh, really had suffered and died, really had been physically resurrected. Underlining this was the fact that the eucharist was celebrated with material elements. The bread and wine, so expressive of body and suffering (and thus so repulsive to the Gnostics) so really represented the essential facts of the incarnate Christ and his cross that they could be described in synonymous and interchangeable terms with Christ's body and blood.

The beginnings of this process are already to be found in Justin. Not only is the eucharist, as has been noted, a means of thanking God for creating the world with all things that are in it. It is also a vivid reminder of the reality of the incarnation. "We do not receive these things as common bread or common drink;" writes Justin, "but just as our Saviour Jesus Christ, being incarnate through the word of God, took flesh and blood for our salvation, so too we have been taught that the food over which thanks has been given by the prayer of the Word who is from him, from which our flesh and blood are fed by transformation, is both the flesh and blood of that incarnate Jesus."[10]

Not surprisingly, many writers have seen in Justin's words evidence for belief in the later doctrine of transubstantiation at an early period in the church's history. But this is to make the mistake of judging early writers out of their historical context. The problems which Justin and the early fathers faced were totally different from those of the scholars of the Middle Ages and more recent times. Support for later positions must therefore only be drawn from these early writers with extreme caution after due weight has been given to the particular environment of the original readers.

Justin is important, however, not only as an example of how the early church tackled the threat of Gnosticism but for his description of the way in which the eucharist was celebrated in the churches with which he was familiar. "On the day called Sun-day," he writes, "an assembly is held in one place of all who live in town or country, and the records of the apostles or writings of the prophets are read for as long as time allows. Then, when the reader has finished, the president in a discourse admonishes and exhorts (us) to imitate these good things. Then we all stand up together and offer prayers; and as we said before, when we have finished praying, bread and wine and water are brought up, and the president likewise offers prayers and thanksgivings to the best of his ability, and the people assent, saying the Amen; and there is a distribution, and everyone participates in (the elements) over which thanks has been given; and they are sent through the deacons to those who are not present. And the wealthy who so desire give what they wish, as each chooses; and what is collected is deposited with the president. He helps orphans and widows, and those who through sickness or any other cause are in need, and those in prison, and strangers sojourning among us; in a word, he takes care of all those who are in need. And we all assemble together on Sun-day, because it is the first day, on which God, having transformed the darkness and matter, made the world; and Jesus Christ our Saviour rose from the dead the same day; for they crucified him the day before Saturday; and the day after Saturday, which is Sun-day, he appeared to his apostles and disciples, and taught them these things which we have presented to you for your consideration."[11]

Here in essence are all the elements of a modern eucharist; the importance of Sunday, the progression through Bible reading and exposition, and intercession, to thanksgiving over the bread and wine, followed by communion and a monetary collection for the sick and needy, to whom the elements are also taken when the main service is finished. But although there is form to the celebration, there is also an appealing informality. "The records of the apostles or writings of the prophets are read *for as long as time allows* . . . *we all* stand up together and offer prayers . . . the president likewise offers prayers and thanksgivings *to the best of his ability*." Elsewhere Justin states that the president wore, "the best and cleanest ordinary garments."[12] Justin and his contemporaries celebrated the eucharist under constant threat of torture and death. Thus their worship reveals an intensity of devotion and spirituality borne of the conviction that through word and sacrament they met the living Christ and fed on him to their eternal well-being.

After the death of Justin in AD 165 the next main second-century writer whose works have survived was Irenaeus. Born in Asia Minor, Irenaeus later travelled west where he became bishop of Lyons in France in AD 177. The need to champion Christian truth against the distortions of the Gnostics led Irenaeus into a new definition of the nature of the eucharistic sacrifice, the effects of which continue to divide Christians to the present day. In the eucharist, he said, "it behoves us to make an oblation to God . . . offering the first-fruits of his own created things. The Church alone offers this pure oblation to the creator, offering to Him, with giving of thanks, from His creation."[13] The Lord himself taught his disciples "to offer God the first-fruits of creation — not as if He Himself had need of them, but in order that they be not ungrateful and unfruitful; when, therefore, he took the oblation of bread, He gave thanks and said: 'This is my body,' and likewise the chalice, which is a product of this earthly creation, He declared it His blood, and made it the oblation of the New Covenant; and thus does the Church . . . offer him to God, Him who is nourishing us; these are the first-fruits of His gifts in the New Covenant."[14]

Hitherto, Christian writers have regarded the eucharistic celebration as a whole as a sacrifice, and have been careful to define the sacrifice in terms of thanksgiving and prayer. For Irenaeus, too, thanksgiving is important ("in order that they be not ungrateful") but the bread and wine, rather than the entire act of celebration, are now the sacrifice, offered as tokens of the body and blood of Christ. And since it is legitimate to speak of the tokens or signs as if they are what they signify, "thus does the Church . . . offer him (i.e. Christ) to God." The eucharist is thus no longer a sacrifice of prayer and thanksgiving alone. It is something else as well. In some sense the bread and wine are offered to God, and in some sense, Christ himself is offered in the bread and wine.

The idea that the bread and wine are offered to God in the eucharist is continued in the *Apostolic Tradition* of Hippolytus. Modern scholars are uncertain who Hippolytus was, but they are generally agreed that his *Apostolic Tradition* reflects eucharistic practice in the church at Rome at the beginning of the third century. As such, the importance of the *Tradition* is unparalleled, for even by that early date the church in the Imperial capital was exercising an influence far beyond the boundaries of the city itself.

In the *Apostolic Tradition* Hippolytus has left two descriptions of a eucharist, one on the consecration of a bishop and the other at a baptism. The idea of sacrifice underlies his whole understanding of the meaning of the eucharist. The bread and wine themselves form the offering whereby God is thanked for his work of salvation in the death and resurrection of Christ.[15] The bread is "the representation, which the Greeks call 'antitype', of the body of Christ"[16] while the cup mixed with wine is "the antitype, which the Greeks call 'likeness', of the blood which was shed for all who have believed in him."[17] Milk and honey are also offered "in fulfilment of the promise made to the fathers . . . 'a land flowing with milk and honey', in which also Christ gave his flesh, through which those who believe are nourished like little children, making the bitterness of the heart sweet by the gentleness of his word."[18] Water is a further offering "to signify the washing, that the inner man also, which is the soul, may receive the same things as the body."[19] However, thanksgiving is still the main motif in Hippolytus' understanding of sacrifice, despite the efforts of some modern scholars to prove otherwise.

Hippolytus, however, is not important merely for his ideas of sacrifice but for the evidence he has left of the form of the eucharistic service, or liturgy, at the beginning of the third century. Features appear for the first time in the *Apostolic Tradition* which indicate a gradual transition from the informal type of celebration described hitherto towards the more rigid type associated with later times.

Thus, the eucharist which follows the consecration of a bishop begins with the presentation of an offering by the deacons to the bishop, "and he, laying his hands on it with all the presbytery, shall give thanks, saying:

The Lord be with you;

and all shall say:

> And with your spirit.
> Up with your hearts.
> We have them with the Lord.
> Let us give thanks to the Lord.
> It is fitting and right.[20]

Next follows the first example of a eucharistic prayer to be found in any extant liturgy. Earlier writers have described the president praying and giving thanks over the bread and the cup and have indicated the lines along which he might be expected to pray. Hippolytus is much more precise, even if his prayer is still only a pattern prayer and not necessarily to be repeated word for word. After Hippolytus the eucharistic prayer becomes the central prayer of the rite, a position it retains in the Catholic tradition of Christianity to the present day. Hippolytus' prayer is therefore worth quoting in full:

> We render thanks to you, O God, through your beloved child Jesus Christ, whom in the last times you sent to us as saviour and redeemer and angel of your will; who is your inseparable Word, through whom you made all things, and in whom you were well pleased. You sent him from heaven into the Virgin's womb; and, conceived in the womb, he was made flesh and was manifested as your Son, being born of the holy Spirit and the Virgin. Fulfilling your will and gaining for you a holy people, he stretched out his hands when he should suffer, that he might release from suffering those who have believed in you.
> And when he was betrayed to voluntary suffering that he might destroy death, and break the bonds of the devil, and tread down hell, and shine upon the righteous, and fix a term, and manifest the resurrection, he took bread and gave thanks to you, saying, "Take, eat; this is my body, which shall be broken for you".

Likewise also the cup, saying, "This is my blood, which is shed for you; when you do this, you make my remembrance".
Remembering therefore his death and resurrection, we offer to you the bread and the cup, giving you thanks because you have held us worthy to stand before you and minister to you. And we ask that you would send your holy Spirit upon the offering of your holy Church; that, gathering them into one, you would grant to all who partake of the holy things (to partake) for the fullness of the holy Spirit and for the strengthening of faith in truth; and, that we may praise and glorify you through your child Jesus Christ, through whom be glory and honour to you, with the holy Spirit, in your holy Church, both now and to the ages of ages. Amen."[21]

Two points in this prayer are particularly worthy of note. The first centres round the clause, "when you do this you make my remembrance." Reference has been made earlier to the view that the purpose of the "remembrance" is to remind God of the death of his Son that the benefits of his death might thereby be made effective in the hearts of the worshippers.[22] When applied to the eucharist the effect of this view is to give the eucharist a propitiatory sacrificial value of itself separate from the propitiatory sacrifice of Calvary, and the eucharist thus becomes far more than a thankoffering. In the 1930s the Anglican Dominican monk Gregory Dix asserted that the particular form which the New Testament words take in Hippolytus' prayer shows that Christ's "command at the Last Supper to 'make the anamnesis of Me' with 'the bread and the cup', is a command 'to stand before Thee and minister as priests to Thee', and this sacrificial character is explicitly brought out in the anaphora."[23] More recently, however, Geoffrey J. Cuming, a member of the Church of England Liturgical Commission, has suggested that the original form of the anamnesis in the eucharistic prayer was simply, as in the New Testament, "Do this for my remembrance."[24] If this is so, it is far less certain that Hippolytus held the sacrificial view of the eucharist which Dix has assigned to him.

The second point to notice in the prayer centres round the plea "that you would send your holy Spirit upon the offering of your holy Church." Fundamental to the teaching of the Eastern Orthodox churches is the idea that in the eucharist the Holy Spirit transforms the bread and wine into the actual body and blood of Christ. Hippolytus' prayer for the descent of the Holy Spirit on the bread and wine has been seen by some as evidence for the beginnings of later Orthodox teaching at an early date. Others have dismissed this part of Hippolytus' prayer altogether, regarding it as a later addition when the idea of transformation by the Holy Spirit was gaining ground. The prayer, however, does not invoke the Holy Spirit to change the elements, but to fill the worshippers "that we may praise and glorify you through your child Jesus Christ." As such, says Cuming, "it seems quite credible."[25]

Besides providing the first example of a eucharistic prayer Hippolytus also describes how the communion was administered:

> When the bishop "breaks the bread, in distributing fragments to each, he shall say:
>
> The bread of heaven in Christ Jesus.
> And he who receives shall answer:
> Amen.
>
> And if there are not enough presbyters, the deacons also shall hold the cups, and stand by in good order and reverence; first, he who holds the water; second, the milk; third, the wine. And they who receive shall taste of each thrice, he who gives it saying:
>
> In God the Father almighty.
>
> And he who receives shall say:
> Amen.
>
> And in the Lord Jesus Christ.
> (Amen).
> And in the holy Spirit and the holy Church.

And he shall say:
  Amen:
So shall it be done with each one."[25]

Hippolytus' eucharist also includes a sermon[26] and care must be taken to ensure that unbelievers do not partake of the elements "unless they first receive baptism. This is the white stone of which John said, 'A new name is written on it, which no-one knows except him who receives the stone.'"[27]

The *Apostolic Tradition* thus marks a time in Christian history when worship was becoming more formal and closely defined than previously. The epiclesis, or invocation to the Holy Spirit to come upon the elements, not as yet to transform them into the body and blood of Christ, nonetheless is preparing the way for later developments in Eastern theology. Equally, the sacrificial character of the eucharist is firmly established and centred in the bread and wine which are offered to God at the heart of the rite. Hippolytus does not follow Irenaeus in identifying the offering with the offering of Christ. Within fifty years, however, that identification will be made more explicitly than ever before by Cyprian, bishop of Carthage in North Africa who will write, "Since we make mention of His passion in all our sacrifices, *for the passion is the Lord's sacrifice which we offer*, we ought to do nothing else than what He did (at the last supper)."[28] Cyprian's assertion will also pass unchallenged for the next fourteen hundred years and will come to dominate eucharistic theology during that period.

In the light of the Jewish and Gnostic claims with which the early church had to contend it is easy to understand why Christian thinking on the eucharist developed in the way it did during the first three centuries. Whether or not those sacrificial categories were right is another matter. Whether or not they should be retained as an indubitable part of Christian teaching long after Jewish ideas of sacrifice and Gnostic distortions have passed away is another matter again. Whether the early fathers were divinely inspired in their writings, faithfully adding to the New Testament revelation truths which must continue to be obeyed by the church in the modern world, or whether they were human and fallible and need therefore to be measured against the New Testament and corrected by it, are further important issues arising from this period. For the foundations of the controversies which continue to divide Catholic and Protestant Christians so deeply were all laid during this earliest period of the church's life, when Christians lived in daily fear of their lives and often laid down their lives because they persisted in celebrating the eucharist and steadfastly refused to recognise Caesar as Lord.

b — *The Edict of Milan and its Effects*

It was this twin persistence in celebrating the eucharist together with refusal to worship the Emperor by casting a perfunctory pinch of incense in the Imperial temple which proved so baffling to the Roman rulers for most of the first three hundred years of the church's life. They simply could not understand why Christians would not perform a simple patriotic act (comparable with today's singing of *God save the Queen* or with the saluting of the American flag). Neither could they understand why Christians were willing to risk death in order to celebrate the eucharist, and why many of them accepted death, bravely and courageously, in successive waves during the first three centuries. But Christians understood that in casting the incense in the Imperial temple they were acknowledging the Emperor as *dominus et deus*, as Lord and God, two titles which they gave to Christ and to no other. Either Christ was Lord and God or the Emperor was Lord and God. They could not both enjoy the same status. And the eucharist was the Christians' positive, weekly affirmation of the Lordship and deity of Christ. No Christian could cast incense in the Imperial temple and remain faithful to Jesus as Lord. No Christian could remain loyal to Christ while willingly absenting himself from the eucharist. That is why when the celebration was over the bread and wine which remained were taken to the sick, that in fellowship with the church they too might feed on Christ to their souls' well-being and their bodies' restoration. That this "reserved sacrament" should have been so abused in later centuries is one of the tragedies of Christian history.

Eventually, dramatically in March 313, the long night of Christian persecution finally ended. Constantine had marched on Rome and seized the Imperial throne from the hands of his rivals. Before the crucial battle of the Milvian Bridge which had made his accession secure he had testified to seeing a flaming cross in the sky surmounted by the words, *in hoc vince*, in this sign conquer! Grateful to the Christ who had granted him victory he passed the Edict of Milan guaranteeing to the church freedom of worship in every respect, together, as with other officially approved religions, generous state assistance in the provision of worship. Whether Constantine actually saw a cross in the sky is doubtful. Probably, as an astute politician, he foresaw the advantage of securing Christian support for his new regime by granting freedom of worship. The effects of his decision were profound and marked a turning-point in Christian history.

First and foremost, Christianity became a public as opposed to a private religion. Although church buildings had begun to be established during the latter half of the third century, Christianity had remained essentially a domestic, private affair, meeting secretly in the homes of its wealthier members, committed to the worship of the risen Lord and the conversion of individuals. With the restoration of its property by the Edict of Milan and generous grants for new property often personally supplemented by the Emperor himself, Christianity rapidly ceased to be domestic and its members soon met exclusively in increasingly splendid and magnificent churches. With this new public image came increased ceremonial and rich vestments. Many have held that these represented an accommodation to paganism by the church's leaders although Gregory Dix has strongly contested this, insisting that all these changes were utilitarian in origin and only attained their later significance with the passage of time.[29]

Nevertheless, the fact that Christian worship rapidly became the public activity of the population at large produced deeper and more fundamental changes in emphasis. The church, for example, became reconciled to the idea of time. While Christians were a persecuted minority they fixed their hope on the world to come. The eucharist was a glorious moment when all the joys of the coming Kingdom of God were experienced in the light of the redemption secured by Christ. But as persecution became an ever-receding and more distant memory, emphasis was placed less on the goal of redemption than on the actual events surrounding its accomplishment. Instead of looking forward, the eucharist thus came to look backwards, and became increasingly a re-enactment before God of the final events of Christ's earthly life.[30]

As more and more, often only half-converted, people flocked into the church, Christian worship began to lose its corporate nature. Before 313 the eucharist was a corporate act in which all members of the church fulfilled their role as members of the body of Christ. The bishop presided, the prophets prophesied, the elders administered, and everyone received the bread and wine. After 313 the clergy became more professional and full-time, and a rapid decline took place in the frequency of lay communion. Instead of being the united action of the whole church the eucharist increasingly became a service said by the clergy to which the laity listened.[31]

These developments in the practical outworking of the eucharist were accompanied by further changes in the church's theological understanding of it as well. As Christians came to look backwards during the celebration to the moment of redemption on the cross rather than looking forward to the return of Christ in glory so the realistic understanding of the eucharistic elements first developed by Irenaeus and Cyprian was increasingly accepted without question. And as the church came to believe more and more firmly that the bread and wine were actually the body and blood of Christ a question was posed which required an answer: how did the bread and wine become the body and blood of Christ? Throughout the church the answer which was given was, by consecration. But in the eastern half of the church, the Holy Spirit was held to effect the consecration, while in the west, the repetition of Christ's words at the Last Supper produced the change.

Thus Cyril, bishop of Jerusalem during the fourth century declared in his lectures to new converts who were waiting to be baptised, "we beseech God, the lover of man, to send forth the Holy Spirit upon (the gifts) set before him, that he may make the bread the body of Christ, and the wine the blood of Christ; for everything that the Holy Spirit has touched, has been sanctified and changed."[32] Meanwhile at Milan in Italy, Ambrose, who was bishop from 374–397 could write:

> Perhaps you will say, "My bread is common (bread)." But that bread is bread before the words of the sacraments; when consecration has been applied, from (being) bread it becomes the flesh of Christ. And by what words and whose sayings does consecration take place? The Lord Jesus'. For all the other things which are said in the earlier parts (of the service) are said by the bishop . . . when the time comes for the venerated sacrament to be accomplished, the bishop no longer uses his own words, but uses the words of Christ. So the word of Christ accomplishes this sacrament.
>
> Before it is consecrated, it is bread; but when the words of Christ are added, it is the body of Christ . . . And before the words of Christ, the cup is full of wine and water; when the words of Christ have been employed, the blood is created which redeems his people. So you see in what ways the word of Christ has power to change everything. Our Lord Jesus himself bore witness that we should receive his body and blood. Ought we to doubt his faith and witness?[33]

This difference between east and west on the issue of consecration marks the beginning of divergence between the two halves of the Catholic church which ultimately led to the Great Schism of 1054 and to the subsequent separate development of the Roman Catholic and Orthodox churches. They continue to disagree on their understanding of the means of consecration to the present day.

As Christian leaders thus asserted the real presence of Christ in the eucharist in increasingly concrete and realistic terms so they spoke of the eucharistic sacrifice in similar realistic vein. After all, if Christ was actually present when the bread and wine were offered to God as his body and blood then Christ was actually offered. So Cyril, while not despising the elements of thanksgiving and praise in the eucharist, also described the offering as "that sacrifice of propitiation, for the common peace of the churches, for the stability of the world, for emperors, or armies and auxiliaries, for those in sickness, for the oppressed."[34] And Ambrose set down the words of the bishop in the eucharistic prayer with which he was familiar: "Remembering his most glorious passion and resurrection from the dead, and ascension into heaven, we offer you this spotless victim, reasonable victim, bloodless victim, this holy bread and this cup of eternal life."[35]

Here is thus a further development. It is not now so much the sacrifice of Christ at the cross which propitiates, or turns away the wrath of God, but the sacrifice of Christ in the eucharist. Christ's earthly sacrifice was offered once.[36] The eucharistic sacrifice is offered repeatedly. If too close an identification is made between the two then almost inevitably the eucharistic sacrifices will come to compromise the unique, historic sacrifice of Christ.

Nor did the Fathers who flourished in the new climate of freedom which the church enjoyed from the fourth century onwards stop at the idea that Christ is offered in the eucharist. Not only is Christ offered, they said, but he offers himself in the eucharist, for the church which makes the eucharistic offering is Christ's body. Thus Ambrose again: "even though Christ no longer seems to be offering sacrifice, nevertheless He Himself is offered in the world wherever Christ's body is offered. Indeed He is shown to be offering in us, since it is His word which sanctifies the sacrifice which we offer."[37] Nor does Christ confine his self-offering to the eucharist. His self-offering is eternal in heaven where, in making constant intercession before the Father Christ is "offering His death on behalf of us all".[38]

In all fairness it must be recognised that not all the later Fathers followed Cyril and Ambrose in their understanding of the eucharist. Chrysostom, the "golden-mouthed" preacher at Antioch from 386–397 and bishop of Constantinople at the turn of the fifth century declared, "Do not think, because you have heard that Jesus is a priest, that He is always offering sacrifice. He offered sacrifice once and for all, and thenceforward he sat down."[39] Theodoret, bishop of Cyrus, a Syrian town north of Antioch, also insisted that in the eucharist, "we do not offer another sacrifice, but accomplish the memorial of that unique and saving one . . . so that in contemplation we recall the figure of the sufferings endured for us."[40] But with the passage of time it was the views of Cyril and Ambrose which prevailed and which were developed in the Middle Ages. Thus the eucharistic offering became more important than Christ's historic offering, and the unique and unrepeatable nature of that offering was largely forgotten in popular understanding. For the great majority of Christian people it was the eucharist, rather than Christ's actual sacrifice which secured forgiveness and the benefits of salvation. Attendance at the eucharist (with infrequent communion) thus became all important. Because the sacrifice was being constantly offered the assurance of salvation which comes through faith in the one perfect, sacrifice of Calvary was lost. The Christian life became a "work" of religious observance instead of an acceptance of the "righteousness of God . . . revealed through faith for faith" (Romans 1:17).

Neither was salvation any more certain for the dead than for the living. From the very beginning of the Christian church those who had died were thought of as sharing in the eucharistic meal with the communicants on earth because they were "away from the body and at home with the Lord" (2 Corinthians 5:8). Such thought is entirely Scriptural. Christians on earth are "surrounded by so great a cloud of witnesses" (Hebrews 12:1). In the eucharist the church may rightly be particularly conscious of the communion of the saints and may rejoice that the church militant and triumphant joins in the meal which is a foretaste of the marriage supper of the Lamb. As time went by it became common practice to recite the names of those who had died in the faith, and particularly to remember those who had endured the supreme test of persecution and martyrdom for Christ. With that practice no-one could quarrel either. Christians have always drawn strength from recalling the faithful in every age; long may they continue so to do. But as the eucharist came to be regarded more as a propitiatory sacrifice than as a thank-offering, and as it came to be seen as a ceremony whereby forgiveness was obtained, so the practice of praying for the departed, that they too might be forgiven and protected by Almighty God was increasingly adopted, and the truth of their eternal forgiveness and perseverance, won for them by the perfect sacrifice of Christ at the cross was increasingly forgotten. The sure and certain hope of eternal salvation became a vain hope that perhaps, if enough prayers were said, and eventually if enough masses were repeated, the departed might one day attain to eternal felicity, but no-one could ever be really sure.

c — Conclusion

The development of eucharistic understanding during the first six hundred years of the church's life makes a fascinating study. It relates to all the life and death issues faced by the early church. It displays Christian leaders grappling with Jewish intransigence, pagan tradition, and the deadly speculations of heretics. These leaders are seen learning to express their faith in terms of the Greek and Roman culture in which they lived, rather than in terms of the Hebrew culture in which Christianity was born. They bowed bloodied heads but refused to submit to cruel persecution. They had to readjust to a pagan empire which suddenly offered friendship and patronage in place of the sword and the stake. Local customs then hardened into universal traditions, and an increasing value was put on uniformity of belief and practice.

The whole process poses a question. Are all of the conclusions to which the Fathers came during those years now a necessary part of authentic Christian doctrine? Must all modern Christians subscribe to them? Or do they need to be tested and judged by the teaching of Christ and his apostles as recorded in the New Testament?

To put the question another way; were the Fathers experiencing the guiding and illuminating of the Holy Spirit who, Jesus promised, would "guide you into all the truth" (John 16:13), or were they human and fallible, engaged in a close combat from which they were not able to stand back and evaluate, unconsciously accommodating the Biblical testimony to the age in which they lived?

Catholic Christians today regard the teaching and practice of the Fathers as an extension of the New Testament, and therefore as binding on the church. This leads them to regard the eucharist as a sacrifice which turns away the wrath of God, the bread and wine "becoming" the body and blood of Christ at the moment of consecration. This in turn leads them to assert that only priests standing in the authentic succession of the Catholic church can effect that change by the words of consecration. The whole process is hallowed by centuries of practice and piety, especially during times when the church stood as a bulwark against barbarism.

Protestants, on the other hand, regard the Fathers with a good deal of scepticism. However much they may recognise the earnestness and courage of second or fifth century leaders, Protestants insist on a rigorous application to their teaching of the test of comparison with the New Testament. When they do so, they are driven to assert that some of the Fathers' conclusions represented a departure from the New Testament rather than an extension thereof.

Protestants find propitiatory sacrifice nowhere but at the cross. They are dubious about "consecration" of the bread and wine, because they find neither the word nor the idea in the New Testament. Of a succession of sacrificing priests they can find no trace in the teaching of Christ and his apostles. They believe that the whole concept militates against a Biblical Gospel of the free grace of God. And since the concept is bound up so closely with the Catholic understanding of the eucharist, it is that rite which was intended to be a sign of unity which tragically becomes the point of division.

CHAPTER THREE NOTES

1 – The *Didache*, chapter 14, quoted in R. C. D. Jasper and G. J. Cuming, *Prayers of the Eucharist: Early and Reformed*, p. 16.
2 – *ibid.*, chapter 9, paragraph 2, quoted in *ibid.*, p. 14.
3 – *ibid.*, chapter 9, paragraph 3, quoted in *ibid.*, p. 14f.

4 – The *Didache*, chapter 10, paragraphs 1–4, quoted in R. C. D. Jasper and G. J. Cuming, *Prayers of the Eucharist: Early and Reformed*, p. 15.
5 – Justin, *Dialogue with Trypho*, chapter 41, paragraph 1, quoted in *ibid.*, p. 17.
6 – See Justin, *ibid.*, chapter 117, paragraph 3, quoted in *ibid.*, p. 18.
7 – Justin, *ibid.*, chapter 117, paragraph 2, quoted in *ibid.*, p. 18.
8 – Quoted in Josef A. Jungmann, *The Early Liturgy*, p. 44.
9 – Origen, *Contra Celsum*, VIII, 57, quoted in Jungmann, *op. cit.*, p. 45.
10 – Justin, *First Apology*, 66.2, quoted in R. C. D. Jasper and G. J. Cuming, *Prayers of the Eucharist: Early and Reformed*, p. 19.
11 – Justin, *ibid.*, 67.3–8, quoted in *ibid.*, pp. 19, 20.
12 – Quoted in A. R. Whitham, *The History of the Christian Church*, chapter 3.
13 – Irenaeus, *Adversus haer.* IV, 18, 4, quoted in Josef A. Jungmann, *The Early Liturgy*, p. 115.
14 – Irenaeus, *ibid.*, IV, 17, 5, quoted in *ibid.*, p. 116.
15 – Geoffrey J. Cuming, *Hippolytus: A Text for Students*, p. 11.
16 – *ibid.*, p. 21.
17 – *ibid.*
18 – *ibid.*
19 – *ibid.*
20 – *ibid.*, p. 10.
21 – *ibid.*, p. 10f.
22 – see above, p. 21f.
23 – Gregory Dix, *The Apostolic Tradition of St Hippolytus*, p. 75.
24 – Cuming, *op. cit.*, p. 11.
25 – *ibid.*, p. 21.
26 – *ibid.*, p. 22.
27 – *ibid.*, p. 23.
28 – Cyprian, *Ep.* lxiii, 17, quoted in Gregory Dix, *The Shape of the Liturgy*, p. 115.
29 – Gregory Dix, *The Shape of the Liturgy*, p. 430.
30 – *ibid.*, p. 305.
31 – *ibid.*, p. 319.
32 – Cyril of Jerusalem, *Lectures*, Lecture 5, paragraph 7, quoted in R. C. D. Jasper and G. J. Cuming, *Prayers of the Eucharist: Early and Reformed*, p. 53.
33 – Ambrose, *On the Sacraments*, Book 4, paragraphs 14, 23, quoted in R. C. D. Jasper and G. J. Cuming, *Prayers of the Eucharist: Early and Reformed*, pp. 98, 99.

34 – Cyril of Jerusalem, *Lectures*, Lecture 5, paragraph 8, quoted in *ibid.*, p. 53.
35 – Ambrose, *On the Sacraments*, Book 4, paragraph 27, quoted in *ibid.*, p. 99.
36 – See above, chapter 3.
37 – Ambrose, *Enarr, in ps. 38*, 25, quoted in J. N. D. Kelly, *Early Christian Doctrines*, p. 453.
38 – *ibid., in ps. 39*, 8, quoted in *ibid.*, p. 453.
39 – Chrysostom, *Homily* on Hebrews 13:9, 10, quoted in ed. J. I. Packer, *Guide-lines*, p. 104.
40 – Theodoret, *In Hebr.* 8, 4f., quoted in J. N. D. Kelly, *op. cit.*, p. 452.

CHAPTER 4 — TRANSUBSTANTIATION AND ALL THAT

Between the end of the sixth and the eighth centuries, the Roman Empire, wracked by decay and barbarian invasions from the north, finally disintegrated and fell apart. Out of the ensuing chaos came mediaeval Europe. During the chaos the Christian church often remained the only stable force within society. So it became a haven, not only for the distressed and insecure, but also for the rich and powerful, who rewarded it for its promise of eternal security with handsome gifts of wealth and land. So the church grew in power and influence, increasingly able to regulate and control, not only every aspect of European religion and society, but every aspect of European politics as well. The bishop of Rome, the Pope, became a political as well as an ecclesiastical leader, the natural successor to the Emperor, ruler of an empire as powerful as the mighty Roman Empire which had fallen to the Vandals and the Goths. Power corrupts: absolute power corrupts absolutely, and during the mediaeval centuries the Papacy became increasingly corrupt, not only in its political and ecclesiastical dealings, but in its religious practices and this nowhere more so than in its understanding and celebration of the eucharist.

a — The Mediaeval Eucharist

The previous chapter showed how, in response to Gnostic heresy, the church was forced into an increasingly materialistic understanding of the presence of Christ in the eucharist and of its propitiatory, sacrificial character. During the early mediaeval period these realistic views were expounded in an ever-increasingly extreme form and widely adopted throughout the western church.

Thus, for example, in 831, Paschasius Radbert, a member of the Benedictine abbey of Corpie in France wrote a treatise *On the Body and Blood of our Lord* for King Charles the Bald in which he declared, "that in the mystery there is real flesh and real blood . . .

and ... though the figure of bread and wine remain, these must be believed to be ... after consecration ... nothing else than the flesh and blood of Christ."[1] A fellow-monk, Ratramn, did protest that Paschasius' views left no room for faith and removed the mystery of the eucharist. He asserted that the change in the elements was not made corporeally but spiritually, but his protest went largely unnoticed.[2] Paschasius' position gained ground to the extent that within a hundred years it was generally believed that in receiving the sacrament the faithful partook of a *portiuncula carnis*, that is, a little portion of the flesh of Christ.[3]

During the eleventh century a further attempt by Berengar, a teacher in the cathedral school of Tours, to secure a more spiritual understanding of the Real Presence was vigorously opposed by Lanfranc, later Archbishop of Canterbury and led, in 1059, to the Council of Rome where the hapless Berengar was forced to retract his views and accept that "the bread and wine which are placed on the altar are after consecration not only a sacrament but also the real body and blood of our Lord Jesus Christ, and that with the senses not only by way of sacrament but in reality these are held and broken by the hands of the priest and are crushed by the teeth of the faithful."[4] One and a half centuries later, in 1215 to be precise, another council, the Fourth Lateran Council, coined a new word to describe the physical transformation of the bread and wine into the body and blood of Christ. That word was transubstantiation.

Along with this physical understanding of Christ's presence in the eucharist went a heightened view of the sacrificial character of the rite, and of its propitiatory effect on God the Father quite independently of Christ's sacrifice on the cross. "Each day in the Mass Christ sheds his blood in this mode to all that believe," declared John Mirk, an English priest, some time during the fourteenth century. Thus the Mass secured for the faithful the same benefits as Christ's continual offering of himself to the Father on the altar in heaven, namely, "remission of sin to all that live here in perfect charity, and ... great succour and release of their pain that (have) been in purgatory." Lest any should doubt that Christ's blood was actually shed in the mass

Mirk told the story of one St Odo, bishop (*sic*) of Canterbury, who was celebrating mass one day together with some priests who did not believe this fact. As Odo broke the bread he saw blood drop therefrom into the chalice and beckoned those who disbelieved to come and see. "And when they saw his fingers bloody and blood ran out of Christ's body into the chalice, they were aghast that for very fear they cried and said: 'Be thou blessed, man, that has this grace just to handle Christ's body! We believe now fully that this is very God's body and his blood that dropped there into the chalice' . . . and so the sacrament turned into this form of bread as it was before."[5]

Here is realism, as applied to the eucharist, complete. The highest service man can give to God, is to celebrate the mass, to offer the sacrifice, to handle and taste the very body and blood of Christ. Hence the haste to enter the priesthood which captivated so many men during the Middle Ages, for to the priest was given the highest honour imaginable, the ability to "make God" upon the altar. For the remainder, not so exalted, they must worship from afar, adoring the exalted host as it was raised for the fraction, and reserved continually thereafter. Notice, they only adored the host and rarely received it, for the Middle Ages not only witnessed profound developments in the way the eucharist was understood but in the way it was celebrated as well.

After the collapse of the Roman Empire liturgical confusion was widespread throughout what had been the Imperial lands. In many places orderly worship virtually disappeared altogether, while in other places widely varying rites were used for different reasons. In time the emergent kings of France and successive bishops of Rome were drawn into increasing political alliance, until on 25 December 800, Pope Leo crowned Charlemagne Emperor in Rome. In gratitude for the honour received Charlemagne determined to restore the Roman liturgy throughout his realm and commissioned Alcuin, master of the cathedral school in York, to accomplish this task.

Alcuin brought to his work the zeal and integrity of a careful and scrupulous scholar. As a result the Roman mass, with only minor local variations, was adopted throughout western Europe for the next seven hundred years. But during those years profound changes occurred in the way it was performed which eventually made it abhorrent to the Reformers of the sixteenth century and produced from them radical, even revolutionary change.

First of all, the eucharistic table, which had once stood in the centre of the worshipping congregation and had then been moved towards the eastern end of the building was now moved so close to the east wall that it became impossible for the celebrant to stand behind it and face the people. Gradually, he was forced to stand in front of the table with his back to the people. At the same time, the table, which had originally been made of wood began to be made of stone and to take on more and more the appearance of an altar. From about 1100 onwards, in Rome, candles began to be placed on the table, and a hundred years later, a crucifix. Further adornments were added during the later mediaeval period.[6]

All of this enhanced the role of the priest who, from being the president of the worshipping and communicating people of God became an intermediary acting on their behalf. For not only did the priest celebrate the eucharist with his back to the people; across the end of the chancel in nearly every church a massive rood screen was built keeping the people in the nave away from the priest and thus away from active participation in the eucharistic action. Not surprisingly, the decline in lay communion which had begun in the fourth century after the accession of Constantine, now gained momentum. For if the bread and wine became the actual body and blood of Christ, who was worthy to handle and receive? The people went to watch, and only occasionally, perhaps three times a year, to receive the bread, while even then the wine was reserved for the priest alone. Thus the note of joyful thanksgiving in the eucharist, so evident in the New Testament and in the early centuries of the church's life, was replaced with an atmosphere of fear and awe.

Because the eucharist became such an awesome affair the priest took to repeating the rite in a low murmur, scarcely audible to the congregation assembled beyond the screen. Latin also remained the language of the liturgy long after it had ceased to be the everyday language of the masses. Thus congregational responses virtually disappeared from the mediaeval eucharist. If the layman could read he took to church his book of devotion for godly contemplation on the Passion of Christ while mass was performed. If he could not read, and the vast majority could not, he simply went to watch. He watched and waited for the surpreme moment of consecration when "Christ" was lifted high and "his body" broken in the fraction. "Lift it higher, O priest! Lift it higher!" he sometimes cried.[7]

Nor did the layman remain satisfied with seeing his "Lord" elevated before the fraction. As the mediaeval period progressed the sacrament, which had long been reserved after the end of the eucharist for carrying to the sick, came to be displayed in a prominent place, on the altar, or above it, or at the side, in an elaborately fashioned tabernacle, that worshippers might adore "Christ" at any time they entered the church. And as the host was thus continually exposed and the practice of lay communion declined the idea gained ground that simply to see the host in this way procured all sorts of benefits.

> That day that thou seest God's body,
> These benefits shalt thou have securely;
> Meat and drink at thy need,
> None shall thee that day be denied;
> Idle oaths and words also
> God forgiveth thee both;
> Sudden death that same day
> Thee dare not dread ('tis true to say);
> Also that day I thee plight [i. e. promise]
> Thou shalt not lose thine eyesight.[8]

The Middle Ages saw the development of the Feast of Corpus Christi, the festival of the blessed sacrament of the body of Christ, and on this day particularly, and at other times also, the host came to be carried about in processions, sometimes with rival processions resulting in riots and bloodshed. The host thus came to be viewed in isolation from the eucharist itself, and became a magic charm protecting from danger and providing a cure for all ills. In the eyes of the people, the host became an idol, to be worshipped and adored.

This magical view of the host, and of the eucharistic rite itself, was emphasised by a further mediaeval development, the practice of private and of votive masses. Private masses originated in the monasteries when too many priests became housed under one roof to be able to celebrate the eucharist for the rest of the community with any degree of regularity. In order not to be deprived of their priestly role these monastic priests began to celebrate by themselves. From the private mass it was a small step to the votive mass, that is, the saying of mass for a particular purpose, cure from sickness, protection on a journey, release from purgatory. As early as 694 a synod at Toledo had had to condemn masses from being said to bring about someone's death,[9] but the practice of votive masses continued and became integral to the mediaeval religious system. Thus, instead of being a means of corporate thanksgiving for blessings secured by Christ, the eucharist became a private means of securing private blessings, and because the priests charged those for whom masses were said, the supposed benefits of the mass were more readily available to the rich than to the poor; they could afford to pay.

If the decline in lay communion, the exposition and adoration of the host and the growth in private and votive masses thus characterised the mediaeval period, the close of the period saw further eucharistic abuses which, in the end, even the Catholic church authorities could tolerate no longer. In some churches so many priests celebrated mass so closely together that their voices conflicted. Other masses were frequently celebrated during Solemn Mass. Masses were said without any assistants. Often no-one, not even the celebrant communicated. Signs of the cross were frantically waved over the host and the chalice as if these contained powers of consecration. Not only the host, but the chalice also, was elevated and displayed on top of the priest's head! Half-corrupt corpses were often laid on the altar. People brought their dogs, falcons and hawks into church with them while mass was being said and frequently chatted with monks and nuns during the celebration.

These are not the exaggerated and carping criticisms of Protestant Reformers intent on destroying the credibility of the Catholic church, but the solemnly recorded admissions of the sixteenth-century Catholic Council of Trent, finally called to bring abuse to an end.[10] But the popular Protestant view that all was corrupt and dark in the mediaeval church before the light of the Reformation dawned is far from the truth. Long before Martin Luther nailed his *Ninety-Five Theses* to the church door in Wittenberg a succession of men and movements had sought to correct error and abuse. Some had operated within the structure of the Catholic church and had seen their views receive official approval. Others had attempted reform but had been rejected and expelled. Since the Papacy demanded that "for every human creature to be subject to the Roman Pope is altogether necessary for salvation,"[11] heresy was a common feature of mediaeval Europe, and a charge of heresy an easy way of dealing with one's enemies. Other would-be reformers welcomed heresy and excommunication and were downright rebels and revolutionaries.

b — Thomas Aquinas and the Summa Theologiae

Thomas of Aquino in Italy was born into a wealthy family in 1226. In time he became a Dominican monk and studied in Paris, then the centre of theological learning in the West. Although nicknamed the "Dumb Ox" by his fellow-students he became the most outstanding theologian of the Middle Ages and must rank with Paul, Augustine and Calvin in possessing one of the greatest intellects ever to be included in the Christian church. His crowning theological achievement, the *Summa Theologiae* has recently been retranslated into English in sixty volumes by a team of American Roman Catholic scholars and perhaps stands as the greatest work of systematic theology and philosophy of all time. Beautifully lucid, warm and profound, the *Summa* deserves to be read, for whether misunderstood or ignored, its influence on Christian thought ever since has been profound.

During the thirteenth century, the philosophy of Aristotle, lost to the West since the fall of the Roman Empire, was finding its way back into the monastic and cathedral schools of Europe from the East, where it had been preserved in the Islamic Empire. It was challenging the monopoly and supremacy of the Catholic church in matters of learning, for Aristotle had taught that all human knowledge originates in the senses, while the church taught that it originates with God. Aquinas accepted Aristotle where natural, human knowledge is concerned but distinguished this from theological knowledge which, he insisted, came by revelation from God and by logical deduction therefrom. Aquinas also insisted that if the doctrine of transubstantiation was undertood in an Aristotelian way it could lift the church's understanding of the presence of Christ in the eucharist away from the crudely realistic categories so widespread in his day to a more spiritual and exalted level.

Aristotle understood reality in terms of "substance" and "accidents". Thus, for example, a table is a table because it possesses the substance of "tableness". All tables possess this substance. That is why they are tables and are recognisable as such. But tables also possess accidents, size, shape, hardness, etc., and so many different kinds of tables exist. Their substance is the same, tableness, but their accidents are different. Similarly, bread is bread because it contains an invisible substance, "breadness", and visible accidents, size, shape, taste, etc. Wine contains the substance of "wineness" and accidents of colour and taste. A human body contains an invisible substance of "bodyness" and visible accidents, arms, legs, eyes, hair and so on.

Thus, for Aquinas, in the eucharist it is the substance of the bread which is changed into the substance of the body of Christ and the substance of the wine which is changed into the substance of the blood of Christ. The change is an invisible change, for the accidents of the bread and wine remain, which is why, in the communion, the elements taste like bread and wine, and not like human flesh and blood.

The Aquinas did not accept the crude realism of the Council of Rome is quite clear at the outset of his discourse on the eucharist: "Christ is not then by bodily presence in the sacrament of the altar."[12] Whatever Aquinas understood by transubstantiation he did not mean that the bread and wine in the eucharist are transformed into the physical body and blood of Christ. That much is clear, and nothing else that he wrote can be wrested to any other conclusion.

"The complete substance of the bread is converted into the complete substance of Christ's body, and the complete substance of the wine into the complete substance of Christ's blood. Hence this change is not a formal change, but a substantial one. It does not belong to the natural kinds of change, and it can be called by a name proper to itself — 'transubstantiation'. . . . It is obvious to our senses that, after the consecration, all the accidents of the bread and wine remain."[13]

Few today would attempt to explain Christ's presence in the eucharist in the terms of Aristotelian philosophy. But to Aquinas, at once thrilled and alarmed by the "new" knowledge from the East it seemed self-evident. Sadly, although Aquinas' teaching was fully accepted by the Catholic church few apparently understood its import, or if they did were prepared to act on it as far as popular understanding of the eucharist was concerned. After all, Aquinas was a scholar and his reasoning had, as it still has, scholarly appeal. It was far too sophisticated for the average unlettered peasant to understand. For him, the concrete categories of the Council of Rome were far more attractive. Furthermore, Aquinas was a scholar who lived before the invention of printing revolutionised communication. Apart from the few who could read his arguments, even fewer could obtain access to the massive tomes of the *Summa*, all of which had to be laboriously copied in classical Latin. Perhaps for that reason it was easy for the leaders of the Catholic church to accept, officially at any rate, Aquinas' teaching. It was distant and remote, and once accepted, posed no real threat to Catholic religion as practised by the majority of the people.

Equally, as with the Real Presence, Aquinas' understanding of the eucharistic sacrifice was far loftier, more spiritual and more scriptural than that propounded by popular priests like John Mirk.

"Is Christ sacrificed in this sacrament?" he asked.

"1. No, it would seem. For it is written in *Hebrews* that *Christ by a single offering has perfected for all time those who are sanctified*. That offering was his sacrifice. Therefore he is not sacrificed in the celebration of this sacrament.

"2. Moreover, Christ's sacrifice was made upon the cross; *He gave himself up for us, a fragrant offering and sacrifice to God*. Now in the mass Christ is not crucified. Neither, then, is he sacrificed.

"3. Again, in Christ's sacrifice *priest and victim are the same*, as Augustine points out. Yet in the mass the priest and the victim are not the same. Therefore the celebration of this sacrament is not a sacrifice of Christ."[14]

Aquinas has become one of the myths of history. To Catholics he is the Angelic Doctor whose theology is eternally valid. To Protestants he is an embodiment of the Antichrist, responsible for all the darkness and superstition associated with their understanding of the hated doctrine of transubstantiation as popularly conceived in the Roman church. In fact, he was neither Angelic Doctor nor Antichrist. Brilliant as he was he was a child of his age and his teaching has to be understood against the philosophical renaissance of the thirteenth century. Catholics today are readier to grapple with this fact than ever before and those who are theologically literate have a far more spiritual understanding of the nature of Christ's presence in the eucharist and of the eucharistic sacrifice than was once the case. Protestants too must rise to the challenge of this new climate of opinion, for as these pages have attempted to show there is little in Aquinas' eucharistic teaching at which they need be offended. At another level, too, Aquinas can receive wholehearted support from Protestants. At the end of his discourse on the presence of Christ in the sacrament Thomas puts his final question and then supplies the answer:

"*Could the body of Christ as it is under this sacrament ever be seen by eye?*

"As long . . . as man is still on the way to heaven, he can only know it by faith, in the same way as other supernatural realities are known."[15]

c — John Wyclif and the English Lollards

If Thomas Aquinas succeeded in interpreting Catholic eucharistic doctrine in a spiritual way and in remaining a loyal son of the Church other mediaeval writers and scholars attempted neither. A hundred years after the Angelic Doctor had left his *Summa Theologiae* unfinished because he felt too unworthy to complete his task, another philosopher began to attract attention with his radical teaching at the newly-established University of Oxford in England. His name was John Wyclif.

By the fourteenth century successive English kings were becoming increasingly restless with their subservient position to the Papacy and were making initially abortive attempts to assert their independence. Wyclif himself, through friends in high places, gradually became more and more involved in this national struggle. John of Gaunt, at that time virtual ruler of England, found him particularly eloquent and convincing in his arguments for the right of the civil government to seize the property of corrupt clergy (of which there was a plentiful supply in fourteenth-century Europe!). For this revolutionary teaching the Oxford philosopher was condemned by the Pope and brought to trial by the church authorities, but popular clamour and political influence protected him. At his trial, a fortuitous earthquake caused his accusers to abandon the charges.

It was at this stage that events took a significant turn. Attacking the corruptions of the church and seeking their reform, Wyclif began to quote the Bible in support of his arguments. To widen the influence of his protest, he translated the Scriptures from the Latin Vulgate (he did not know Hebrew or Greek) into the English language. This in turn led him to reflect more seriously on their contents for his own spiritual instruction. The effect was devastating. In 1378, a year after his condemnation by the Pope he could still claim to be merely a reformer, not a "heretic", and specifically accepted the doctrine of transubstantiation as popularly understood, which was increasingly becoming the accepted test of religious orthodoxy. Three years later he was writing his scathing *De Eucharistia*.

"There has never been a heresy more cunningly smuggled into the church than transubstantiation," he wrote.[16] He presented four arguments against "this veritable abomination of desolation in the holy place".[17] First, it is contrary to Scripture. Second, it is unsupported by early church tradition. "Since the year of our Lord one thousand, all the doctors have been in error about the sacrament on the altar, except perhaps Bérengar of Tours."[18] Thirdly, it is plainly opposed to the testimony of the senses. Finally, it is based upon false reasoning. "How canst thou, O priest, who art but a man, make thy Maker? What! the thing that groweth in the fields — that ear which thou pluckest today, shall be God tomorrow! As thou canst not make the works which he made, how shall ye make him who made the works?"[19]

He realised, of course, how drastic an approach this was, and how horrifying it must sound. He hastened to add that he still believed in the Real Presence, and to maintain this he propounded the idea of Remanence — that the bread remains bread after consecration, but to it is added the body of Christ, so that, "in the consecrated host there remains the body of Christ, truly and really."[20] "Yet I dare not say that the body of Christ is essentially, substantially, corporeally or identically that bread."[21] And by saying that, he denied transubstantiation as clearly as when he roundly abused it.

This frontal attack on one of the foundations of mediaeval Christendom shocked many of Wyclif's erstwhile friends. What he was denying was the central awesome mystery of the church, by which the priests controlled the dispensing of eternal life. To uncover ecclesiastical corruption was a popular English pastime, but to deny the central mystery of religion was a very different thing. Wyclif found himself deserted by his political friends, shouldered out of public affairs and increasingly isolated.

Yet there was an inexorable logic in the way the reformer's mind was led. Once he began to test the claims of the church by the standards of Scripture, the whole centre of gravity of his religion was shifted. It is in this context that his struggle must be understood. From now onwards, however it had begun, his protest against the power of the clergy was an attack on men whose pretensions no longer had any basis. By the exclusive claim to the performance of the miracle of the mass, "the lowliest priest was raised high above princes."[22] But if the miracle was a sham, the claims of the miracle-worker were false. In turn, the attack on transubstantiation was not the exercise of a philosopher who thought he had a better theory than Aquinas'. Wyclif saw the whole question, what happens to the bread and wine, as an enormous red herring across the path of true religion. "Nothing is more repulsive than that any priest in celebrating daily makes the Body of Christ," he wrote indignantly,[23] because nothing could be worse than to draw the mind of the worshipper and the penitent in the wrong direction. Not grace mediated by a priestly miracle, but grace streaming from the eternal God was the source of the Christian's hope. Not a visible church hierarchy with immense pomp and power, but an invisible church of God's elect, chosen by his grace; this was the new centre of Wyclif's thinking. "We do not worship a recent God," he thundered (i.e. one just "made" on the altar).[24]

John Wyclif never suffered either the imprisonment or the martyrdom which he expected and almost invited. Disorder and schism in the church in Europe drew the attention of his enemies away from him, and it was only after his death that the Council of Constance condemned him as a heretic. His body was exhumed and burned, and the ashes thrown into a local stream in his parish of Lutterworth in Leicestershire. But no such posthumous revenge could close the Pandora's box which Wyclif had opened with his attack on transubstantiation.

The first effect was, of course, in England itself. Wyclif's Bible, so painfully and dangerously translated and copied, had a dynamic effect upon the restless society of the fourteenth century. Already excited by the quarrels of their betters (the very throne was in doubt), the rebellion of their equals (Wat Tyler's peasant revolt shook the country) and the incoherence of their priests (who could not even decide on the identity of the Pope), the people now found themselves in actual possession of the Scriptures in their own language. The effect was electric. One contemporary claimed, with understandable exaggeration, "you could not meet two persons on the highway but one of them was Wyclif's disciple."[25]

One consequence was the Lollard movement. The meaning of the name is obscure. Literally it implied, "someone who mutters". It may have referred to the habit of reluctantly muttering the responses at public worship with a mental reservation that it was all nonsense, or it may have referred to the secret passing-on of the forbidden message. At first seeking to reform the church from within, the Lollards maintained that the principal task of a priest is to preach the Gospel, not to celebrate a mystery. Persecution inevitably followed, and Lollardry became an underground sect with its own ordained ministers. The "Lollard's Tower" in Lambeth Palace, the home of the Archbishop of Canterbury, was often filled with imprisoned heretics, and one of their carvings can still be seen on the wall, proclaiming, "Jesus amor meus", Jesus is my love. Many of them were hanged or burned for that love.

In spite of the violence of the opposition Lollardry was never completely blotted out. It flowed on, in secret, like an underground stream, with occasional appearances above ground, throughout the fifteenth and sixteenth centuries, when, two hundred years after Wyclif's death and one hundred and thirty years after its first martyrdom, it merged with the main stream of Protestantism The Lollards' *Twelve Conclusions*, published in 1394 showed them to be as opposed to transubstantiation as Wyclif himself had been:

1. Christ never instituted the Roman priesthood . . .
4. The pretended miracle of the sacrament of bread drives all men but a few to idolatry, because they think that the body of Christ which is now in heaven can, by the power of the priest's word, be enclosed essentially in a little bread which they show the people.[26]

d — The Mediaeval Underground

The English Lollards were part of a stream of protest which spanned the countries of Europe throughout the mediaeval period. Often led by colourful and bizzare characters the protesters were united in their opposition to what they regarded as the arrogant claims of the Roman church and the idea of sacramental manipulation as expressed in the eucharist. Instead of salvation by gazing on the uplifted host or the reserved sacrament these protesters propounded the idea of salvation by believing response to the preached word of God. Thus, like Wyclif, many were concerned to translate the Bible into their native language.

Peter Waldo, for example, was a French merchant who experienced a sudden conversion about the year 1175, as a result of which he gave away his possessions and devoted himself to a life of poverty and preaching. Remnants of older movements and likeminded dissenters gathered around him to form a lay movement very similar to the later Franciscans, and for a time it had papal approval. However, Waldo took the significant step of translating the Bible and although he himself later faded from view, the word Waldensian began to be used almost indiscriminately of any "heresy" which challenged the Catholic Church and denied the miracle of transubstantiation. Waldensians received both the bread and wine at the eucharist and regarded the rite as merely a remembrance of the Lord's body given for them, and at the same time as a strong exhortation to yield themselves to be broken and poured out for his sake.

Two hundred years later, Jan Hus, rector of the university of Prague, led another protest movement. The teaching of Wyclif, at that time being condemned and suppressed, leap-frogged into eastern Europe through the movement of scholars. Hus embraced some of Wyclif's teachings, wrote tracts of his own which contain many exact verbal parallels, and publicly welcomed Lollard leaders. He administered communion in both kinds, and produced the first-ever translation of the Bible from Hebrew and Greek texts into a European language. He gained an immense following, and combined national desires for independence with attacks on the corruption of the Catholic clergy and the sale of indulgences.

The student coming to the story for the first time may feel it has a familiar ring. He will realise, that in many of its details, it will soon be repeated again in the events surrounding the life of Martin Luther. But did Hus in fact deny the doctrine of transubstantiation? The first charge against him at the trial which led to his execution was precisely that he did. But the trial was a farce. With the help of a good lawyer he would have been acquitted. In less hysterical circumstances he would never have been tried. The truth seems to be that he put the Scriptures alongside the sacraments in a way thought to be "heretical" in mediaeval times, and that he tried to express what takes place at the eucharist in a less mediaeval way.

The irony is that Wyclif who really was a "heretic" escaped the martyrdom which he almost invited, whilst Hus, who was simply a reforming Catholic, was martyred as a heretic. There is a revival of interest in his writings today, for he prompts the question: If reformers like Hus had been heeded in time, would the Protestant Reformation ever have taken place?

Catholic historians have painted the mediaeval period as an age of faith when Christendom was united under one church, loyally supported by the people of Europe. Such a picture is far from the truth. Waldo, Wyclif and Hus were only the giants among a whole host of protesters who aimed to remain distinctively Christian and indeed to reform the Catholic church. In addition there were dissidents who denied the Trinity, radicals who despised marriage, mystics who taught a totally individualistic religion, dualists who denied the Incarnation, preachers who dismissed the Bible. They had nothing in common except a revolt against the Catholic church. Nevertheless, there is indisputable evidence of a constant and often interconnected "evangelical" revolt against sacramentalism as portrayed in the Catholic mass. "In all the centuries before the Reformation . . . one could not live out the span of an average human life without experiencing at first hand that not all people believed in the so-called miracle of the mass. . . . Indeed, salvation by believing response to the preached Word and salvation by sacramental manipulation lay in mortal combat with each other all through mediaeval times."[27]

CHAPTER FOUR NOTES

1 – Paschasius Radbert — *De Corpore et Sanguine Domini*, quoted in C. W. Dugmore, *The Mass and the English Reformers*, p. 26.
2 – Ratramn's argument is summarised and quoted in Dugmore, *op. cit.*, pp. 28, 29.
3 – See Dugmore, *op. cit.*, p. 33.
4 – Quoted in Dugmore, *op. cit.*, p. 34.
5 – See *Mirk's Festial: a collection of Homilies by Johannes Mirkus (John Mirk)*, ed. T. Erbe (E.E.T.S., Extra series, XCVI), London 1905. A summary of and quotations from this sermon are found in C. W. Dugmore, *The Mass and the English Reformers*, pp. 76–78.
6 – See Theodore Klauser, *A Short History of the Western Liturgy*, pp. 97–101.
7 – Gregory Dix, *The Shape of the Liturgy*, pp. 14, 620.
8 – John Mirk, *Instructions for Parish Priests*, ed. E. Peacock, London 1868, quoted in C. W. Dugmore, *The Mass and the English Reformers*, p. 70.
9 – See Yngve Brilioth, *Eucharistic Faith and Practice: Evangelical and Catholic*, pp. 84, 85.
10 – See Joseph M. Powers, *Eucharistic Theology*, p. 32.
11 – See C. W. Dugmore, *The Mass and the English Reformers*, p. 80
12 – Thomas Aquinas, *Summa Theologiae*, 1965 trans., Vol. 58, p. 55.
13 – *ibid.*, Vol. 58, pp. 73, 75.
14 – *ibid.*, Vol. 59, pp. 133–135.
15 – *ibid.*, Vol. 58, p. 117.
16 – Merle d'Aubigné, *The Reformation in England*, p. 92.
17 – *ibid.*
18 – *ibid.*, p. 93.
19 – *ibid.*
20 – Quoted in Boorman, *Reformers before the Reformation*, p. 91.
21 – *ibid.*, p. 92.

22 – Green, *A Short History of the English People*, p. 596.
23 – John Wyclif, *De Eucharistia*, 100:1, quoted in C. Bullock, *The Story of England's Church*, p. 158.
24 – *ibid.*, p. 159.
25 – Merle d'Aubigné, *The Reformation in England*, p. 90.
26 – David Boorman, *Reformers Before the Reformation*, p. 94.
27 – Leonard Verduin, *The Reformers and their Stepchildren*, pp. 146, 153.

CHAPTER 5 — REFORMATION AND DIVISION

The Protestant Reformation of the sixteenth century tore Christendom apart, ended the Middle Ages, created the political concept of the independent state, encouraged the idea that common people may rebel against their rulers, and hastened the rise of Capitalism. All of this happened because a few outstanding Christian leaders began to ask pressing questions about how a man can get right with God, and what happens when a priest says the words of blessing over bread and wine. So closely interwoven are men's religious beliefs and their basic approaches to the whole of life.

The book which precipitated the Reformation was the Bible, quickly translated into the tongues of ordinary people, and for the first time made available in great numbers by the marvellous innovation of the printing press. Until that happened, learning was almost exclusively in the hands of priests, and the priests claimed the awesome power of bringing God down upon the altar in the miracle of the Mass. When the Bible fell into the hands of the people it raised questions about that claim and the whole philosophy behind it. Men began to discover that the book which their church proclaimed to be divinely inspired and infallible, taught doctrines which that same church regarded as deadly error, and cast doubts on claims which that same church regarded as fundamental.

The great front-line figures of the Reformation were Martin Luther of Germany, Ulrich Zwingli of Switzerland and John Calvin of France. They were the architects who built the future, and their different approaches to the eucharist in particular have continued to influence Protestant theology to the present day. They succeeded in their protests where Wyclif and Hus and others like them had failed, not only because printing ensured the rapid widespread dissemination of their views, but also because all over northern Europe, restive "Catholic" rulers were breaking away from the Papal Empire, and gave them protection from the political arm of the church which, a century earlier, would have ensured their rapid demise. Luther was first in the field, Zwingli reacted strongly against him, and Calvin tried to mediate.

a — Martin Luther and Ubiquity

The story of the brilliant German law student turned monk, priest and lecturer in Biblical theology who shook mediaeval Catholicism to its depths by nailing his *Ninety-Five Theses* on the church door of Wittenberg on All Souls' Day 1517 and thus started the Reformation, has been amply told elsewhere.[1] Suffice to say that that initial colourful act was never the work of a revolutionary intent on destroying the one visible Church of Christ on earth, but the careful academic response of a university professor using the accepted means available to scholars of his day of opening a learned debate on the sale of indulgences. What happened as a result took Martin Luther completely by surprise.

Reared in the Catholic church of northern Germany, young Martin Luther quickly learned that salvation was a matter of attending mass, saying prayers, confessing sins to a priest and doing the prescribed penance. The trouble was, the medicine failed to heal his tender, troubled conscience despite his taking it in ever stronger and stronger doses by entering an Order, going on pilgrimage to Rome and observing his religious duties ever more punctiliously. But the Order put Martin in the university and made him lecturer in theology and charged him with the task of explaining the Bible to his students. And so it was, that after years of inner struggle Luther found the peace and forgiveness for which he was looking, not in an ecclesiastical system of duties, penalties and rewards but in simple, believing acceptance of the free grace of God offered him in Christ. "The just shall live by faith" (Romans 1: 17 AV) became his creed and his tortured pilgrimage to peace with God seemed over.

However, in early sixteenth-century Europe the entire Roman Catholic church, both universal and local, was being financed by the sale of indulgences. In response to contrition for and confession of sin, and a contribution to some worthy need of the church, indulgences were granted which reduced the soul's expectancy of time in purgatory after death before heaven was entered by a given number of years. Thus, forgiveness was dispensed by the church and was only available at a price. By 1516 Luther was protesting against the practice as it existed locally in and around Wittenberg. John Tetzel's arrival, in 1517, selling indulgences to finance the rebuilding of St Peter's basilica in Rome, finally sparked the *Ninety-Five Theses* and the Reformation. For if Luther thought he was only opening an academic debate, the nature of his protest struck so fundamentally at the basis of the mediaeval church as to make debate impossible. "Every true Christian, living or dead, partakes of all the benefits of Christ," proclaimed the thirty-seventh thesis with the implication that the purchase of indulgences was unnecessary for forgiveness. "The true treasure of the Church is the pure Gospel of the glory of God," announced the sixty-second, and not remission of time in purgatory by indulgences. And once Luther had openly attacked the financial basis of the mediaeval church and its connection with forgiveness it became but a short step to attack the whole sacramental basis of the church whereby it claimed a monopoly in the means of the dispensing of Divine grace.

Within three years of his attack on indulgences Martin Luther published *The Babylonian Captivity of the Church*, his primary work on the sacraments and their enslavement by the church. With characteristic forthrightness he reduced the number of sacraments from seven (confirmation, marriage, ordination, penance, extreme unction, mass and baptism) to two (mass and baptism), the two that had been instituted by Jesus himself. By dispensing with ordination Luther attacked the privileged position of the Roman clergy (who were thus no longer necessary for the dispensing of Divine grace) and prepared the way for the concept of the priesthood of all believers. He also prepared the way for the transformation of the mass to the Lord's Supper, for if ordination was no longer a sacrament a duly ordained priest was no longer necessary to procure the benefits of the eucharistic sacrament. In other words, it was no longer the priest who "made God" on the altar by the magical repetition of the Dominical words of institution, but the faith of the believer which apprehended Christ's mystical presence in the bread and wine.

For while Luther totally rejected the mediaeval doctrine of transubstantiation as popularly understood, his literal understanding of Jesus' words, "This is my body. . . . This is my blood," never allowed him to reject the notion of the real, objective presence of Christ in the eucharist. To explain this he continued the mediaeval debate begun by Aquinas and the Schoolmen. Instead of the substance of the bread and wine becoming the substance of the body and blood of Christ, Luther argued that the consecrated elements are both Christ's body and blood *and* bread and wine. That the substances of body and blood and bread and wine should thus be joined together seemed perfectly feasible in view of the way in which fire and iron are joined together in red-hot iron. "Why should not Christ be able to include his body within the substance of bread, as well as within the accidents?" he asked.[2] And to avoid the charge that this doctrine of "consubstantiation" involved the localisation of the body of Christ on the altar in the way that transubstantiation had done, Luther asserted the concept of Ubiquity. Christ's body can be both at God's right hand and on the altar because "Scripture teaches that God's right hand is not a place in which a body might be situated, as on a golden throne, but is God's almighty power, which at once cannot be in any place, and yet must be in every place."[3] This concept was particularly useful in the way it established both the transcendance and the immanence of God in Christ, but in continuing to explain the Real Presence in mediaeval categories Luther was at his most unsatisfactory. The net effect of his teaching was to make the Presence even more baffling than it had been before.[4]

By denying the sacrament of ordination, however, Luther not only placed the emphasis on faith instead of on the priest to apprehend Christ in the eucharist. He also removed the complete mediaeval difference between the ways in which the priest and the people observed the eucharist. As has already been described in the previous chapter, the end of the Middle Ages saw the culmination of a process which had begun as early as the fourth century, whereby the priest alone received communion while the people merely sat and watched, and even when the people did receive, the cup was reserved for the priest. With Luther all that changed. "No mass without communicants," became his unyielding principle.[5] In the early days of the Reformation this insistence on communion was accompanied by a profound understanding of the idea that through communion believers are united with Christ and with the faithful in every land and in every age. Later controversy forced Luther to concentrate on the individualistic aspects of communion; communion became the means whereby the individual accepts Christ by faith. Communion must therefore be preceded by penitence, so, like the Catholic mass before it, from being a joyous occasion the eucharist became solemn and awesome. In course of time, too, the eucharist ceased to be the central act of worship of the Lutheran church, and this to its continuing impoverishment. Nevertheless, for all its shortcomings, the restoration of communion was one of the most positive and lasting benefits of the Lutheran Reformation.

So Luther made faith the means of grace, denied transubstantiation and restored communion for all to the eucharist. He also rescued theology from the impasse it had reached at the end of the Middle Ages whereby the one, unique, historical sacrifice of Christ at the cross was repeated every time mass was said. Luther simply cut the Gordian knot. Christ was not sacrificed in the eucharist. He was present, to be sure, and all the benefits of his sacrifice were available to the believer, but Christ himself was not sacrificed. "What then shall we offer?" he asked. "Ourselves, all that we have with constant prayer; and as we say, Thy will be done on earth as it is in heaven ... So too we are to offer him our thanks and praise for his unspeakably sweet grace and mercy, which he has promised and given to us in this sacrament."[6] This self-offering is an offering together with Christ. "In this sense it is permissible and right to call the mass a sacrifice, not indeed in itself, but as the means whereby we offer up ourselves together with Christ; that is to say, that we cast ourselves upon Christ with a sure faith in his testament, to come before God with our prayer, our praise, and our oblation, only through him and his mediation, believing firmly that he is our Shepherd and our Priest in heaven before the face of God."[7]

All this, however, needed constantly explaining if the people were ever to escape from their corrupt understanding of the eucharist in which they had been held throughout the mediaeval period. Fundamental therefore to the Lutheran eucharist was the exposition of the Word. To Luther the Word was not merely the Bible because "the gospel is really not that which is contained in books and composed in letters, but rather an oral preaching and a living word, a voice which resounds throughout the whole world and is publicly proclaimed."[8] Thus the Word was proclaimed through the Bible and through the sacrament, the two complementing each other that Christ might be received by faith. "These people do not know and see who say that it doesn't make sense that Christ should be in bread and wine. Of course Christ is with me in prison and the martyr's death, else where should I be? He is truly present there with the Word, yet not in the same sense as in the sacrament, because he has attached his body and blood to the Word and in bread and wine is bodily to be received."[9]

In 1523 events finally forced Martin Luther to make his own revision of the Roman mass. Initially in Latin and only with reluctance translated into German, Luther's *Formulae Missae* retained the shape and structure of the Roman mass as far as possible. The actual canon, or central prayer, of the mass was omitted because of its direct reference to sacrifice, and communion was to be administered to all the people in both kinds. The sermon became more prominent but otherwise all the elements of the Roman mass remained: bowings, vestments, veerings to the altar or to the audience, lectern and pulpit on opposite sides of the church, even for a further nineteen years elevation of the elements. This had the effect of drawing attention to the omissions as much as to the inclusions, and a negative impression was given. The *Deutsche Messe* looked what it was — a hatchet job!

Later generations of Reformers would thus condemn the Lutheran Reformation for being too half-hearted. The form (and name) of the mass was retained, something suspiciously akin to transubstantiation was preserved and ministers continued to look like sacrificing priests. Nevertheless, these priests could marry and thus share with the people the joys and cares of family life. In turn the people shared in communion with their priest. If the Lutheran Reformation was half-hearted it nonetheless remained within the authentic Christian tradition and secured an initial breakthrough from the shackles of mediaeval Catholicism. On that achievement others would be able to build.

b — *Ulrich Zwingli and Memorialism*

While Martin Luther was guiding the course of the Reformation in Germany a young priest in training was coming quite independently to similar views in Switzerland. Through the study of Erasmus' Greek text of the New Testament Ulrich Zwingli adopted Reformed views and threw himself, with ravenous zeal, into the task of getting to know the Bible. He wrote out all of Paul's letters word by word, and made a written summary of the four Gospels. With mounting excitement he grasped what could be achieved by systematically preaching the Scriptures in a church just beginning to discover their wonders. When, at the age of thirty-five, he was appointed people's priest at Zurich Minster he immediately put the idea into action. The pulpit of those days provided all that a combination of television, radio, newspapers, theatre and political meetings provide in the twentieth century. In the minster pulpit Zwingli announced his intention of preaching consecutively, verse by verse, through the whole New Testament, interspersing the four Gospels between groups of epistles. It had, as one city councillor drily observed, the virtue of being a novel idea.

That was in 1518, and the preacher, as good as his word, plunged into an exposition of the list of names at the beginning of Matthew's Gospel. It was the sheer novelty which captured people's imagination, and soon the minster was thronged for every sermon. Zwingli was no orator, but he preached with deep earnestness and great authority. Before long he had the whole of German Switzerland stirred by his ideas. A public debate was called by the city council in 1523. It was the sixteenth-century equivalent of the kind of public enquiry which might be convened in the twentieth century to consider objections to a proposed new motorway. At the debate Zwingli presented sixty-seven propositions, rather like Luther's ninety-five theses, but with a different purpose. His aim was to capture the assent of the council to his new ideas and to gain its support for the radical reformation of the church. He succeeded. On 12 April 1525, the council, by a small majority, voted to end the Roman services. The following Maundy Thursday, on the anniversary of the institution of the Lord's Supper, a movable wooden table was set up in the nave of the minster. On it were spread wooden platters and tumblers. Christ's words of institution were recited without comment, and the bread and wine were offered to all who came to receive. The Reformation had triumphed. Its leader had only five years to live.

Despite his triumph, however, Zwingli was in a difficult position. If he had initially come to reformed views independently of Luther, he was now well aware of the German's teaching and position. Luther had been excommunicated from the Roman church; Zwingli was still one of its recognised, ordained priests. On the one hand he enjoyed the precarious support of a divided city council. On the other hand he was being pressured by radicals dissatisfied with what they considered to be the half-hearted course of the German Reformation. Foremost amongst these was Andreas Carlstadt, a one-time associate of Luther now taking refuge in Zurich. He suggested that when Jesus said, "This is my body," at the Last Supper, he was pointing to himself and not to the bread; a dubious proposition, but a sign of the direction of radical thought. Other more extreme radicals were rejecting infant baptism and abominating any sacrificial interpretation of the mass. The ancient voice of "mediaeval heresy" was being raised once more, only now it was expecting to be heard.

As Zwingli came to a settled position on the eucharist he was also deeply, if unconsciously, influenced by something else, the philosophical presuppositions he brought to his thought. Without denying the supernatural character of the Christian faith or its divinely-revealed content, Zwingli was concerned that it should conform to the tenets of human reason. In other words he was a kind of Christian rationalist. He was also a realist. That is to say he believed that physical objects and universal concepts have a real existence outside the human mind. In all of this he was deeply at odds with Martin Luther. Luther had been deeply influenced by the teaching of the fourteenth-century scholar William of Occam. William had argued that the true basis of reality is found only in the human mind, and that because God's real existence cannot be proved it can be known only by faith. Faith thus transcends reason and the Christian faith need not therefore be bound by rational tenets.

William of Occam's thought is known as Nominalism and Luther's adoption of it enabled him to assert the concept of Ubiquity, the idea that Christ is both in heaven and in the bread and wine on the eucharistic table, for he could see nothing impossible in this idea. Zwingli, on the other hand, would have none of this. Christ could not be both in heaven and in the bread and wine, for that is unreasonable. Christ is in heaven and there he must remain. Christ's words at the Last Supper, "hoc est corpus meum," "this is my body," must therefore mean, "hoc significat corpus meum," "this signifies my body." And as Zwingli interpreted the Last Supper by John 6 he found plenty of support for his conclusion. For did not verse 63 ("It is the spirit that gives life, the flesh is of no avail") demonstrate that when the chapter commanded to eat Christ's flesh and to drink his blood, it was a spiritual, and not a literal, eating that was required? And did not verse 64 ("But there are some of you that do not believe") demonstrate that the command to eat Christ's flesh and to drink his blood was in effect a command to believe in his Passion?

All this seemed self-evident and eminently reasonable to Zwingli but it did not leave him without problems. For despite his insistence that Christ was in heaven Zwingli had to recognise that he is on earth as well, and in order to explain Christ's earthly presence Zwingli resorted to the curious device of separating Christ's divinity from his humanity. In heaven Christ was present only in his humanity, that is, in his ascended body, while on earth Christ was present in his divinity. Yet despite all the problems associated with the self-emptying of Christ (see Philippians 2:5–8), Christ's dual nature cannot be separated in this way. Christ is both God and man, at once fully human and divine. In his risen body he was worshipped as God (see John 20:28) and in that same body he ascended into heaven where "he reflects the glory of God and bears the very stamp of his nature, upholding the universe by his word of power" (Hebrews 1:3). Scripture gives not a shred of support to Zwingli's separation of Christ's divinity and his humanity as different modes of his presence in the world and in heaven. Indeed, Zwingli almost fell back into the old Gnostic heresy of separating spirit from matter and of making spirit altogether good and matter altogether evil, for it was inconceivable to him that Christ in his divinity could indwell material objects such as bread and wine.

Zwingli's restriction of Christ's human presence to heaven left him with another problem, for it made heaven a place rather than a state descriptive of God's presence. It thus enabled Luther to reply, with great cogency, that from such "childish thoughts it necessarily follows that they fix God also to one place in heaven, on a golden throne. Apart from Christ there is no God, and where Christ is, there the Godhead is wholly."[10]

Zwingli's eucharistic teaching finally led to a far more radical break with Rome than did Luther's. Where Martin retained the essential form of the mass with only its objectionable features omitted, Ulrich abandoned it altogether. His Zurich Rite of 1525 began with a sermon and continued with a prayer to accomplish rightly the "praise and thanksgiving which thy only Son our Lord and Saviour Jesus Christ commanded us, the faithful, to make in memory of his death." This was followed by 1 Corinthians 11:20–29, the *Gloria* and John 6:47–53. Next the Apostles' Creed was recited and the deacon exhorted the people to receive the communion with trust, faith and confidence in the Lord Jesus Christ. A further prayer preceded the words of the institution, the communion and the recitation of Psalm 113. Finally, the celebrant dismissed the congregation with the words,

"We thank thee, O Lord, for all thy gifts and thy goodness, who livest and reignest, God for ever and ever." "Amen." "Go in peace."[11]

The Zurich Rite was to have a far more profound effect on future generations than Zwingli could possibly have realised that fateful Maundy Thursday in 1525. For by putting the sermon right at the beginning of the rite and the communion almost at the end, word and sacrament were placed, by implication at least, in virtual opposition to each other. Indeed, Zwingli's satisfaction with a mere four celebrations each year sharpened this separation. Indeed, the eucharist virtually ceased to be a sacrament at all. It conveyed no grace, but was merely a memorial of Christ's death, celebrated in obedience to Christ's command, "Do this in remembrance of me." Later generations would make the word paramount, and many would rarely receive communion in the glad and joyful spirit of thanksgiving so apparent in the early church.

Meanwhile in Germany, Martin Luther, harassed by radicals, horrified by the Peasants' War, harried by German nobles, and seeing the movement for reform beginning to splinter was furious with his Swiss co-religionists. Under great pressure from friends anxious to preserve Protestant unity, he agreed with reluctance to meet the Swiss brethren for consultation. They eventually met in Marburg in 1529 under the chairmanship of Prince Philip of Hesse. Luther brought Melanchthon and Brem; Zwingli was accompanied by Oecolampadius and Bucer. At last the great teachers of reform were meeting face-to-face. Luther made a bad start by dismissing Bucer with the curt words, "You are from the evil one! There can be no harmony between us!"

Nevertheless, they hammered out massive areas of agreement. On subjects as diverse as the Trinity, justification, infant baptism and the rejection of purgatory they were completely at one, a fact remarkable enough in the context of religious controversy and new-found freedom then prevailing. But when they opened the subject of the eucharist they reached an impasse. With typical Teutonic stubbornness Luther chalked dramatically on the table between them the words, "*hoc est corpus meum*" — This is my body — and refused to move an inch from his understanding of what they meant, silently pointing to them as the reply to every suggestion made by the Swiss. Zwingli burst into tears.

The discussion continued, but constantly came to grief over the same problem. For Luther the eucharist was basically a sacrament administering grace; for Zwingli it was basically a symbol or sign of grace already given. For Luther, the words of the liturgy (spoken in faith) achieved a change in the elements, bringing a strengthening of life to those who received them in faith, and damnation to those who received in unbelief. To Zwingli, if faith was not present in the recipient, he received neither good nor harm, for he was only eating bread. At one stage Zwingli was willing to accept the suggestion that the body of Christ was present, really present, represented by the bread, for the believer, but he could not accept the further idea that Christ was present, irrespective of faith.[12] The Colloquy of Marburg broke up with a joint statement on what the reformers held in common, but nothing could hide the fact that the Reformation was divided.

In recent years Zwingli's teaching on the eucharist has been parodied as the doctrine of the Real Absence,[13] but this is to do him less than justice and to neglect his rich teaching on faith. The year after Marburg, Zwingli produced his final statement of belief. In it he stated, "I believe that in the holy communion the true body of Christ is present in the mind of the believer . . . But that the actual real body of Christ is present in the communion or is consumed by our mouth and teeth as is maintained by the papists and some who long for the flesh pots of Egypt, is something that we not only deny but we consistently maintain that it is an error and contrary to the Scriptures."[14] Thus, Zwingli did not totally exclude Christ's presence in the eucharist, but he restricted it to the grateful conscious remembrance of his death in the mind of the believer.

In 1531, two years after Marburg, Zwingli was killed as an army chaplain on the battlefield of Kappel. He and Luther had stood at two ends of a spectrum. At one end is the actual bodily presence of Christ in the eucharist. At the other is the necessity of faith. In the thirty years which followed Zwingli's death a shy, young scholar from Paris attempted to take a middle position.

c — John Calvin and Virtualism

Born at Noyon in France in 1509 John Calvin studied at Orleans, Bourges and Paris where, in 1533, he first discovered the teaching of Martin Luther. A sudden conversion followed, and three years later the first edition of Calvin's *magnum opus*, *The Institutes of the Christian Religion*, appeared. By expounding the Apostles' Creed the newly-converted scholar aimed to show that the Protestant faith was truly Christian despite its break with Rome.

The next year, 1537, John Calvin stayed overnight in Geneva on a journey. The leading reformer in the city was Guillaume Farel, a fierce, red-headed, prophetic figure with the discernment and humility to see that in spite of all his efforts Geneva's change of mind was no change of heart. Catholicism had been cheerfully abandoned for a mixture of political and immoral reasons, but nothing like a New Testament church had begun to appear. In Calvin, Farel saw the man who could achieve lasting reform and when he naturally enough declined Farel's urgings to stay and help, the older man stood before him with upraised hand and invoked God's curse on the young scholar's studies and writings should he continue to refuse. Thus began Calvin's turbulent, twenty-eight year relationship with the Swiss city, a relationship which made Geneva the spiritual centre of Reformed Christianity with a profound and continuing influence on Holland, Switzerland, Scotland, South Africa and the United States of America to the present day. Successively enlarged in subsequent editions *The Institutes of the Christian Religion* became one of the most influential religious texts of modern Europe and one of the most profound Christian classics of all time.

From those years in Geneva John Calvin has often been portrayed as a bigot, an extremist and a dictator. In fact he was none of these, and his approach to the eucharist illustrates this. As in so many other matters Calvin was no innovator, but sought a middle way between the earlier Reformers, just as long as there was that full obedience to the Word of God which was the touchstone of all his thinking.

Calvin was no dictator, for the Genevan authorities did not always accept his suggestions and often he had to bow to their will. He was no bigot nor extremist for "he favoured a liberal practice of intercommunion between churches. He besought the English refugees at Wesel not to desert the communion of the Lutheran church. Fellowship with Lutherans, Anglicans, Waldensians, Bohemian Brethren was cherished by him. He unhesitantly admitted that some within the Church of Rome were God's elect. His passion for ecumenical unity induced an ecclesiastical tolerance that was unusual in his day, and is distasteful to many in our own day."[15]

Calvin was deeply grieved at the sharp differences inherited from Luther and Zwingli. On the whole he blamed Luther. He wrote pointedly that stubborn repetition of the words, "This is my body," settles nothing, and listed similar statements of Jesus acknowledged to be figurative.[16] He had no time for Ubiquity; an invisible omnipresent body is not a body at all in any meaningful sense.[17]

What had Calvin to contribute, then, to the eucharistic debate? Essentially, he took a mediating position. The body of Christ is indeed in heaven, but the virtue of his death is made available in the sacrament. Those who partake feed on Christ, eat his flesh and drink his blood. The Christ who is in heaven is mediated to the believer by the Holy Spirit. Calvin simply put in juxtaposition the various strands of scriptural teaching.

"After God has once received us into his family, it is not that he may regard us in the light of servants but of sons, performing the part of a kind and anxious parent, and providing for our maintenance during the whole course of our lives . . . To this end, he has given another sacrament to his Church by the hand of his only begotten Son — viz. a spiritual feast, at which Christ testifies that he himself is living bread (John vi. 51), on which our souls feed, for a true and blessed immortality . . . The signs are bread and wine, which represent the invisible food which we receive from the body and blood of Christ . . . The body which was once offered for our salvation we are enjoined to take and eat, that, while we see ourselves made partakers of it, we may safely conclude that the virtue of that death will be efficacious in us. Hence he terms the cup the covenant in his blood. For the convenant which he once sanctioned by his blood he in a manner renews, or rather continues, in so far as regards the confirmation of our faith, as often as he stretches forth his sacred blood as drink to us."[18]

Thus, "by means of the gospel, and more clearly by the sacred Supper, . . . Christ offers himself to us with all his blessings, and we receive him in faith."[19] This reception by faith is, however, more real and positive than Zwingli was prepared to allow. "According to them to eat is merely to believe; while I maintain that the flesh of Christ is eaten by believing, because it is made ours by faith, and that that eating is the effect and fruit of faith; or, if you will have it more clearly, according to them eating is faith, whereas it rather seems to me to be a consequence of faith . . . In this way, the Lord was pleased, by calling himself the bread of life, not only to teach that our salvation is treasured up in the faith of his death and resurrection, but also, by virtue of true communication with him, his life passed into us and becomes ours, just as bread when taken for food gives vigour to the body."[20]

As to the precise mode of Christ's presence in the eucharist Calvin is careful to avoid definition. "The sum is, that the flesh and blood of Christ feed our souls just as bread and wine maintain and support our corporeal life . . . This could not be, did not Christ truly form one with us, and refresh us by the eating of his flesh, and the drinking of his blood. But though it seems an incredible thing that the flesh of Christ, while at such a distance from us in respect of place, should be food to us, let us remember how far the secret virtue of the Holy Spirit surpasses all our conceptions, and how foolish it is to wish to measure its immensity by our feeble capacity. Therefore, what our mind does not comprehend let faith conceive, viz. that the Spirit truly unites things separated by space . . . The bond of that connection (i.e. being one with Christ) is the Spirit of Christ, who unites us to him, and is a kind of channel by which everything that Christ has and is, is derived to us."[21]

In the *Institutes* Calvin was free to expound his understanding of the eucharist without any restriction. When it came to the actual mode of celebrating the rite he was less successful. On his arrival in Geneva in 1537 Zwingli's Strasbourg rite was already in use and Calvin had to accept this. Like Zwingli, he was convinced of the necessity of the Word in the eucharist. "There cannot be a right administration of the Supper without the word," he declared. "Any utility which we derive from the Supper requires the word. Whether we are to be confirmed in faith, or exercised in confession, or aroused to duty, there is need of preaching."[22]

Unlike Zwingli, Calvin was not satisfied with quarterly or even monthly communions. "The sacrament might be celebrated in the most becoming manner, if it were dispensed to the Church very frequently, at least once a week. The commencement should be with public prayer, next, a sermon should be delivered; then the minister, having placed bread and wine on the table, should read the institution of the Supper. He should next explain the promises which are therein given; and, at the same time, keep back from communion all those who are debarred by the prohibition of the Lord. He should afterwards pray that the Lord, with the kindness with which he has bestowed this sacred food upon us, would also form and instruct us to receive it with faith and gratitude; and, as we are of ourselves unworthy, would make us worthy of the feast by his mercy. Here, either a psalm should be sung, or something read, while the faithful, in order, communicate at the sacred feast, the minister breaking the bread, and giving it to the people. The Supper being ended, an exhortation should be given to sincere faith, and confession of faith, to charity, and lives becoming Christians. Lastly, thanks should be offered, and the praises of God should be sung. This being done, the Church should be dismissed in peace."[23] In all this, however, Calvin never got his way, and quarterly communions rapidly became the norm at Geneva, and later, throughout Reformed Christianity.

From Geneva, under the leadership of John Knox, the Reformation was carried to Scotland, where, in time, in its Presbyterian form, it became the established faith of the country. Knox's *Book of Common Order* (1564) and the *Directory for the Public Worship of God* (1644) became the standard liturgical texts of the Scottish church and the basis of Presbyterian worship worldwide. According to the latter, the celebration of the sacrament is to be announced a week beforehand. During the week the elders are required to visit every member of their congregation with metal tokens inscribed with the words "Do this in remembrance of me". On the day itself communicants are to be warned of the dangers of unworthy participation, but also encouraged if they repent of their sins. The elements are blessed, the Pauline words of institution are recited, the central eucharistic prayer follows and the communicants are served, seated at tables to recall the setting of the Last Supper. A short exhortation and final thanksgiving conclude the service.

Thus the shy, young Paris scholar, who intended to stay overnight in Geneva and stayed for twenty-eight years, continues to influence the celebration of the eucharist throughout the world. Where Luther had made communion integral to the eucharist, Calvin also included the preaching of the Word. Sadly, however, his failure to achieve weekly communions in Geneva has had the unforeseen effect in Reformed Christianity as a whole, of setting the Word against the sacrament and of exalting the former at the sacrament's expense. With that development Calvin would have profoundly disagreed. Another unforeseen development followed from Calvin's teaching as well. His requirement that communicants should be made worthy to receive the sacrament was overemphasised by his followers with the result that Reformed communions became solemn and awesome occasions instead of glad and joyous festivals of thanksgivings. Indeed, so paramount did the idea of worth become that the truth of justification by faith, on which Calvin's teaching and his experience of God was founded, came close to being obscured and lost. Happily, in today's ecumenical climate, healthy correctives are being made to these trends. Even weekly communions are being introduced in some congregations.

d — Thomas Cranmer and Receptionism

If the Genevan Reformation was to have the widest immediate influence, the English Reformation in the sixteenth century was to have longer-term effect because what happened in the kingdom of the Tudors was to have global repercussions.

The events in England can never be understood unless it is grasped that there were two distinct reformations, often overlapping, but flowing from different sources and pursuing different aims. There was a political reformation centred in the person of the monarch. There was a spiritual reformation springing from the influence of the English Bible.

Henry VIII, who used Parliament to pass the Acts of Supremacy and thereby to become Supreme Head of the Church of England, cared little whether men in general are justified by faith. He cared a great deal more whether he, in particular, was justified in marrying Anne Boleyn. But even after his quarrel with the Pope, Henry was a bad Catholic rather than a good Protestant. To the end of his days he dutifully burned an occasional "heretic", and at the end it was to the Catholic last rites that he entrusted his soul.

The religious reformation, which ran parallel with Henry's seizure of the headship of the English church, was the direct result of the impact of a Bible in the language of the people. For that, William Tyndale gave his life. Men of his calibre, with preachers like Thomas Bilney and Hugh Latimer, were brought into liberty of conscience and assurance of salvation because they abandoned what they regarded as the priestcraft, penances and pilgrimages of the church for the promises of God in Christ and his finished work on the cross. It was the familiar dilemma which had been faced by the best of the mediaeval heretics, by Hus in Prague and Luther in Germany, and earlier, by Wyclif in their own land. On one side stood a sacramental religion which, as a matter of plain fact, kept the Bible from the people, and as a matter of their own experience could not give assurance. On the other side stood an open Bible and a simple Gospel to be preached and believed. Inevitably, they saw the Mass as the epitome of the sacramental religion they decided to abandon.

The two halves of the English Reformation coalesced in the enigmatic figure of the Archbishop of Canterbury, Thomas Cranmer.

His story was a convoluted one. At times he appeared to be the typical worldly priest, ever ready to serve the interests of his master the king, always able to adjust the law of the land and the tradition of the church to accommodate him. In this respect he looked rather shabby beside the Chancellor, Sir Thomas More, who lost his head rather than compromise his Catholic conscience. Yet Cranmer himself eventually died a heroic death for firmly Protestant principles, dying at the stake for his opposition to a Catholic queen.

Just exactly what Cranmer's final position was with regard to the eucharist is curiously hard to define — a remarkable fact when it is borne in mind that he was given the responsibility for shaping the liturgy and the Prayer Book of the Church of England. Certainly he abandoned transubstantiation and the sacrificial aspect of the Mass. Modern writers have variously summed up his position as Zwinglianism and a doctrine of the Real Absence,[24] Calvinism and virtualism[25] and a kind of Augustinian reformed Catholicism.[26] The difficulty is to understand what he meant by the Real Presence in the eucharist.

> Really, carnally and corporally Christ is only in heaven, from whence he shall come to judge the quick and the dead,[27] *Cranmer wrote*. And since a body can be in only one place at a time, the bread and wine remain bread and wine, before, during and after the eucharist. Yet when the elements are received and eaten by believers, then Christ is truly present to their spiritual health and protection.
>
> Thus our Saviour Christ knowing us to be in this world, as it were, but babes and weaklings in faith, hath ordained sensible signs and tokens, whereby to allure and draw us to more strength and more constant faith in him. So that the eating and drinking of this sacramental bread and wine is, as it were, a showing of Christ before our eyes, a smelling of him with our noses, a feeling and groping of him with our hands, and an eating, chewing, digesting and feeding upon him to our spiritual health and protection.[28]

These were startling enough words, and are very far from a doctrine of absence. Cranmer was concerned that communicants should exercise faith, not simply in a past historical event (the cross), but in a living Christ who came to them and was truly present as the elements of bread and wine were received. Yet it was in the act of communion, not in the elements themselves, that Christ was present. Thus, Cranmer could say, "It is my constant faith and belief that we receive Christ in the sacrament verily and truly."[29] As to how exactly that happened Cranmer maintained very much the same reverent agnosticism as Calvin. The Real Presence was indeed real; it was to be known by faith, and its mode was not a subject for conjecture. This has been the classic position of the Church of England ever since, eloquently re-stated later in the sixteenth century by Richard Hooker, and again in the eighteenth century by Daniel Waterland.[30]

As far as any notion of sacrifice in the Mass was concerned, the Archbishop was adamant: "One kind of sacrifice there is, which is called a propitiatory or merciful sacrifice, that is to say, such a sacrifice as pacifieth God's wrath and indignation, and obtaineth mercy and forgiveness for all our sins . . . which is the death of the Son of God our Lord Jesus Christ; nor never was any other sacrifice propitiatory at any time, nor never shall be."[31]

For that insistence, Cranmer eventually went to the stake during the reign of Queen Mary. Yet at the same time he was quite happy with the concept of Christian obedience and devotion being referred to as a sacrifice.

> Another kind of sacrifice there is, which doth not reconcile us to God, but is made of them that be reconciled by Christ, to testify our duties unto God, and to show ourselves thankful unto him; and therefore they be called sacrifices of laud, praise, and thanksgiving.
>
> The first kind of sacrifice Christ offered to God for us; the second kind we ourselves offer to God by Christ.
>
> And by the first kind of sacrifice Christ offered also us unto

his Father; and by the second we offer ourselves and all that we have, unto him and his Father.

And this sacrifice generally is our whole obedience unto God, in keeping his laws and commandments.[32]

During the brief reign of Edward VI, from 1548 to 1553, Thomas Cranmer was able to seize a unique opportunity to realise his life's ambition, and in so doing to produce his most lasting memorial, *The Book of Common Prayer*. For by the death of Henry VIII the Archbishop had come to the conclusion that since in the Mass "is manifest wickedness and idolatry, wherein the priest alone maketh oblation satisfactory, and applieth the same for the quick and the dead at his will and pleasure; all such popish masses are to be clearly taken away out of Christian Churches, and the true use of the Lord's Supper is to be restored again, wherein godly people assembled together may receive the sacrament every man for himself, to declare that he remembereth what benefit he hath received by the death of Christ, and to testify that he is a member of Christ's body, fed with his flesh, and drinking his blood spiritually."[33]

This restoration of the "true use of the Lord's Supper" was achieved in three stages. First of all, in 1548, a set of new English devotions was inserted bodily into the text of the Latin Mass. Secondly, in 1549, the first Prayer Book appeared, in which the structure of the Mass was retained but all references to the offering of the sacrifice of Christ, to the bread and wine as the people's oblations, and to the corporeal presence of Christ in the elements were removed. Regular communion by the people as well as the priest was also prescribed, and the people were to receive both the bread and the wine.

Thirdly, in 1552, the second Prayer Book was published and therein Cranmer's views received their full liturgical expression. In this the shape of the Mass was abandoned along with every reference in the service capable of receiving a Catholic interpretation. Furthermore, the structure of the new rite came to its climax in the act of communion, not in the moment of consecration as in the Mass. Thus the altar became a table situated lengthwise in the chancel or even the body of the church that the communicants might sit and kneel around it. The priest repeated Jesus' words at the Last Supper without any movement of his hands over the bread and wine. Even the words of administration of the 1549 rite, "the Body of our Lord Jesus Christ, which was given for thee, preserve thy body and soul unto everlasting life . . . the blood of our Lord Jesus Christ, which was shed for thee, preserve thy body and soul unto everlasting life," were abandoned in favour of the simpler formulae, "take and eat this in remembrance that Christ died for thee, and feed on him in thy heart by faith with thanksgiving . . . Drink this in remembrance that Christ's Blood was shed for thee, and be thankful."

The 1552 Prayer Book was the "only effective attempt ever made to give liturgical expression to the doctrine of justification by faith alone,"[34] yet Cranmer failed in his reforms and in his intentions. His failure was partly popular, partly political and partly ecclesiastical. Cranmer intended to replace Mass with communion, the adoration of the host by the people with the distribution of bread and wine among the people, but he failed to reckon with the inherent conservatism of the English people. After half a millennium and more of just watching the eucharist and occasionally receiving the bread, they simply refused to accept Cranmer's prescription of a weekly communion, and often the priest was left to communicate on his own while the worshippers remained in their places and watched.

Cranmer also reckoned on a long reign by the boy king Edward VI, but the year after the publication of the 1552 Book the young monarch finally succumbed to yet another of the many illnesses which had dogged his brief reign and died. A futile attempt to maintain a Protestant succession in the person of Lady Jane Grey lasted but ten days before the Catholic Mary Tudor ascended the throne. The mass was restored, the Prayer Books were banned, Bishops Latimer and Ridley and Archbishop Cranmer himself went to the stake, and a witch-hunt began throughout the nation to mete the same fate on any others who continued to hold Protestant views. That policy earned the queen the title of "Bloody Mary" and the country sighed with relief when, after a mere five years, her reign too ended in an early decease.

Elizabeth became queen in 1558 believing she could solve the country's religious quarrels and unite Catholic and Protestant with a typical English compromise. A third Prayer Book was published using much of Cranmer's material but, in the eucharist, combining the Catholic words of administration of the 1549 rite with the Protestant words of the 1552 rite. The result was cumbersome, to say the least. Nor did Elizabeth's policy succeed, for both Catholics and extreme Protestants were dissatisfied with her 1559 Book. Sixty years later Archbishop Laud replaced the communion table along the east wall and fenced it with rails. Ostensibly, this was to keep dogs from fouling it (!) but the practical effect was to take eucharistic worship a step towards a Catholic style of worship with the people having to be summoned from the nave to the communion rail to receive the bread and wine. Another forty years later, the Act of Uniformity and Book of Common Prayer of 1662 restored manual acts to the consecration of the elements. Its demand that services should be conducted only as prescribed in the Prayer Book drove a further wave of Protestant ministers out of the Church of England.

Thus 1552 was "an ill-starred book" but the present writers cannot share Bishop Frere's contention that in it "English religion reached its low water-mark."[35] Both Elizabeth and Charles II followed Cranmer's structure and used most of his material. Modern Anglican liturgies have retained many of his most beautiful prayers. The Book of Common Prayer of 1662 has become part of the literary heritage of English-speaking people around the world with a continuing spiritual appeal for thousands of worshippers. And while there will always be many sincere and devout Christians who will not find a spiritual home in the Church of England, the Anglican Communion probably includes a wider variety of Christians representing the whole Catholic-Protestant spectrum than any other Christian tradition. In a day when Christians of all traditions are seeking greater ecumenical understanding of each other, that is no small achievement and for it Thomas Cranmer, Catholic archbishop, Protestant convert and Christian martyr can take some of the credit.

e — English Dissent

As has already been hinted, Elizabeth's religious settlement and the Act of Uniformity of 1559 did not meet with the universal acceptance for which she had hoped. To Catholics, the settlement failed to bring the English church back into the fold of Rome, while to many Protestants it failed to make the church fully reformed. The most extreme of the Protestants rejected the settlement root and branch. From the outset they refused to obey the requirement of the Act of Uniformity to worship God in the parish church according to the formularies of the Book of Common Prayer, and insisted on meeting separately in homes, in woods, in fields, wherever it might be convenient. For their convictions many of these early Separatists were persecuted and executed by servants of a queen who regarded religious conformity and political loyalty as one and the same thing. Yet from their ranks the Congregationalists and Baptists of the nineteenth and twentieth centuries are descended.

The Separatists rejected the Elizabethan settlement on the grounds that it equated the English nation with the Christian church. "All this people were in one day, with the blast of Queen Elizabeth's trumpet, of ignorant papists and gross idolaters, made faithful Christians,"[36] wrote Henry Barrowe, a persistent critic of the regime. But the church, to the Separatists, was not the English people, but a community of "visible saints" gathered to worship the Christ who promised, "where two or three are gathered in my name, there am I in the midst of them" (Matthew 18:20). Thus, the Church of England was a counterfeit church and its sacraments, *ipso facto*, were counterfeit as well. It "cast the precious body and blood of Christ to hogs and dogs,"[37] and if visible saints communed in the parish church with "papists, atheists, whoremasters and drunkards",[38] then they were proclaiming a one-ness with non-Christians which made the sacrament a nonsense, a "unity of sin".[39] For, "the Lord's Supper is a seal of our partaking and growing together in one body, whereof Christ is the head."[40]

Not only were the sacraments spurious, however, because they were the product of a counterfeit church. They were also suspect, in the eyes of the Separatists, because the Act of Uniformity and the Book of Common Prayer required them to be celebrated according to a fixed liturgy. Such a requirement was a nonsense. It was a denial of the sovereignty of the Holy Spirit and of the sufficiency of Scripture. Men leading worship because they were called of God and recognised by their fellows could be relied upon to say the right things without resort to dubious liturgies devised by bishops in a corrupt church whose office could not be found in the New Testament but was derived from popish tradition. This is what the Separatists felt and they said it with their usual frankness. Not surprisingly, in an England where, for most of her reign, the Queen was desperately strengthening her grip on the throne against the plots and machinations of many enemies at home and abroad, many of the Separatists were hunted from pillar to post. Magistrates sent constables to break up the solemn gatherings of earnest Christians. Ruinous fines were imposed. Many rotted in prisons where basic necessities were denied them, and their dependants went without food. As Elizabeth's policy was followed by her Stuart successors many sought exile in welcoming Holland. Others set out across the Atlantic in tiny ships, facing terrors on the journey and worse at their destination, to hammer out of a hostile wilderness a new society where they could enjoy the luxury of meeting undisturbed with visible saints. Of those who remained in England an increasing number died in prison or on the gallows. Their one desire was a pure church where valid sacraments united obvious Christians.

Not every Protestant in sixteenth-century England, however, followed the extreme action and violent language of the Separatists. Many, equally unhappy with the Elizabethan settlement because it did not go far enough in its reformation of the church, decided to stay within its ranks and work for further reform, or purification, from inside. For over a hundred years, from 1559, these "Puritans" gradually extended their influence and power within the national church. They attempted to change its system of government from bishops to elders. In so doing they founded English Presbyterianism, today united with Congregationalism into the United Reformed Church. In worship and particularly in their celebration of the sacraments they attempted to give practical expression to their profound Calvinism. Curiously, in so doing, they so exalted the minister's role in the service, and gave such a subservient listening role to the people, that in the style of the eucharist, they almost returned to the mass to which they were so staunchly opposed.

For instance, the Puritans' enthusiasm for the Protestant principle, "no sacrament without the Word", led them to insist that the minister who administered the sacrament must also be the preacher. The effect of this was to concentrate leadership of worship on the ordained clergyman and to make him, to all intents and purposes, into a priest. The Puritans would have stoutly denied this conclusion, but this was the practical effect of their action. So insistent were the Puritans on this principle that many of them considered it was better not to receive communion at all than to receive it at the hands of one who was not ordained to preach, and this, together with a shortage of ministers, made infrequent communion very common, as it has remained in English nonconformity to the present day.

Secondly, the Puritans introduced the concept of "worth" into the reception of communion. Only those who were "worthy" could receive, and elaborate lists were drawn up of those who should be denied the bread and wine, the flagrantly immoral, for example, and the persistently quarrelsome. The trouble was, of course, that the exercise of this discipline fell to the minister who thus had to make it his business to be aware of the personal behaviour of the members of his congregation. Again, the practical effect of this was to give the minister a position in the community similar to the pre-Reformation Roman priest. Furthermore, while the principle of "worth" had been introduced with the best of intentions in an age as notorious for loose living as today's, it ultimately led to a practical denial of the Reformation principle of justification by faith. Puritan religion became a religion of works, and the sacrament, instead of being a sacrament of forgiveness and thanksgiving, became a reward for a holy life. Even when it was infrequently celebrated many of the congregation would leave before the actual communion, or would fail to receive the bread and wine because they did not feel they were sufficiently "worthy". This again marked a step in the mediaeval Catholic direction of eucharist without communion.

Thirdly, the Puritan concentration of the leadership of worship in the person of the minister, and their insistence on the primacy of the Word led them into celebrating long, wordy eucharists in which the minister did all the talking while the congregation listened passively. It was little different from the Catholic practice where the priest recited the rite whilst the people watched from a distance. The Puritan principle is best seen in the Reformed Liturgy of Richard Baxter, published in the middle of the seventeenth century. Baxter was a warm-hearted, moderate Puritan whose ministry completely transformed the West Midlands town of Kidderminster and his Reformed Liturgy was produced in an abortive attempt to stave off the expulsion of Puritan ministers from the Church of England.

The rite began with an Instruction (read or preached extempore) covering Creation, the Fall, the Incarnation and the Crucifixion. Then followed an Exhortation of nine hundred words, which was succeeded by a Prayer of Confession of seven hundred words, with seventy Scripture references provided! The acts and words of Consecration followed at last, but in no part of the service until they received the elements did the worshippers say or do anything. Then followed several more prayers, including one of five hundred words with fifty Scripture references, which might be followed by a hymn (something else at last for the worshipper to do!) and an exhortatory sermon, "if there be time"![41] It was almost as if Jesus had commanded, "*believe* this . . ." or "*understand* this . . ." or "*say* this . . ." rather than "*do* this in remembrance of me."

Of course it is not really fair to compare Puritan worship too closely with its Catholic counterpart. The Puritans themselves would have roundly denied the comparison and, indeed, never tired of denouncing popery and the mass in their lengthy sermons and exhortations. Their enthusiasm for the Bible was infectious and many of them filled their churches to suffocation every week. In the eucharist they attempted to focus attention on the great central verities of the Christian faith by stripping away mercilessly all the accumulations of traditional rites and ceremonies which, they considered, had almost smothered its essential meaning. Candles and incense, vestments and jewels, choirs and processions were all thrown out. The Word was read and the Supper was eaten. The minister stood where he was visible, said words that were intelligible, broke bread, poured out wine, and invited the people to eat and drink. In austere solemnity, with perhaps rather too much monologue, public worship did what it is surely intended to do; it set forth Christ, in word and simple action, before the minds of believing people.

In the outcome, the Puritan attempt to complete the reformation of the Church of England failed. Briefly, from 1649 to 1660, after the end of the Civil War and throughout the Protectorate of Oliver Cromwell, the Puritans had their way, but the nation refused their brand of disciplined religion. In 1660 the monarchy was restored, a new Act of Uniformity and Book of Common Prayer were passed through Parliament, and all ministers were required to promise the use of its services and no others by St Bartholomew's Day, 1662. Two thousand Puritan ministers refused to comply and so were ejected from the national church along with many of their congregations. A period of intense persecution followed but the Puritan tradition proved too strong to destroy, and dissent, or nonconformity as it came to be called, became a permanent feature of English national life.

In fact the enforced addition of many of the national church's finest clergy to the ranks of the "dissenters" guaranteed the survival of Separatism, which was no longer maintained by a tiny minority of Independents and Baptists. Many of their new allies (moderate Anglicans and Presbyterians) now found themselves warmly in sympathy with a Christian movement which virtually ignored liturgy altogether. The virtues of such a liturgy, they began to suspect, were not now very obvious. The trenchant pen of John Owen pointed out that if liturgy was designed to promote unity, it had done exactly the opposite; if it is designed to preserve the true faith, it is odd that it has to be so often altered; and if it comes from God Himself, it is puzzling to see men before our eyes devising it and haggling over it as they go along.

"For my part, I know not anything that ever obtained a practice and observation amongst Christians, whose springs are more dark and obscure than those of liturgies ... In things which concern the worship of God, the commanding power is Christ, and His command is the adequate rule."[42] Moreover, "God hath graciously promised his Holy Spirit as a Spirit of grace and supplications unto them that do believe, enabling them to pray according to His mind and will."[43] Prayer is a spiritual exercise not to be regulated by human devices.

This kind of argument was the really distinctive contribution of non-conformity. It went back beyond the most ancient liturgies and posed the question of their *origin* and therefore their *propriety*. Whilst Protestants and Catholics contended about the correct formulae and the valid sacraments, Free Churchmen questioned the need for formulae at all, and demanded to know what was meant by "valid". For although a certain casualness about the Lord's Supper gradually crept in amongst the dissenters, by and large it was true to say that they observed the sacrament with reverence and deep piety, that their gatherings (whether for preaching or for sacrament) were marked by many tokens of the presence and activity of God, and that as individuals they maintained a standard of sincere Christianity, zeal for the Gospel and devotion to Christ way in advance of that displayed by the average member of the "established" church. "Chapel-folk be more hand-in-glove with Them Above than we," admits the Anglican churchgoer, Joseph, in Hardy's *Far from the Madding Crowd*; it was an idea widely accepted in seventeeth to nineteenth-century England, and there was a good deal of evidence for it. Bernard Manning puts it a little more technically when he describes his Congregational forefathers as "restating the meaning of churchmanship ... showing in actual practice that the grace of God was not confined by legal processes... In austere solemnity, setting forth Christ once again in Word and Sacrament."

If pressed as to what *did* constitute validity, all of them would reply, in effect — the presence of Christ which he solemnly promised to all who gather in his name — symbolised by the simple elements of the Sacrament, authorised by the solemn and believing attention given to God's Word, and evidenced by the obvious work of the Holy Spirit in confirming faith, giving assurance, raising the heart in worship, and transforming the character. What more could be asked?

Of course there was the danger that such an *inward* attitude might lead to them dispensing with the outward forms of worship altogether. That is precisely what happened with the Quakers. But most dissenters were preserved from that excess simply because of their determined loyalty to Scripture. The Bible ordained the Sacraments; that was enough for them. Baptists went further than most others in the Quaker direction, without actually falling over that precipice, precisely because they clung to their Bible as the confirmation and correction of inward experience. "The outward baptism and supper do not confer and convey grace... but as the word is preached, they serve only to support and stir up repentance and faith... The outward supper (which only baptized persons must partake) presents and figures that spiritual supper... in the communion of the Spirit"[44] wrote John Smyth in 1610, the first English Baptist pastor.

It was to be a strong strand of super-Zwinglian teaching throughout Baptist history. The popular Victorian preacher Dr Alexander Maclaren of Manchester could declare in 1884, "All our theories about the meaning and value of this Communion Service must be found within the four corners of that word... a memorial rite, and as far as I know, nothing more whatsoever."[45]

This emphasis led many Baptists into an individualistic understanding of their faith with profound consequences for their theology of the eucharist. The most famous of these ejected Baptists was John Bunyan, author of many books including the timeless allegory, *The Pilgrim's Progress*. In this great classic there is little place for the

Communion Service, and when it is mentioned (and this is the subtle development) it is recommended merely as a personal help to the believer, a means to an end. In Part Two of the book young Matthew, Christiana's son, is given some tablets to ward off poisoning after eating forbidden fruit. The pills are made "ex carne et sanguine Christi. The Latin I borrow," Bunyan admits modestly.[46] It is not really clear whether he is allegorising the Lord's Supper, or the cross, or the former as an application of the latter. In any case, the pills are for Matthew's benefit, and that is all.

Elsewhere in his works, Bunyan describes baptism and the eucharist as "shadowish and figurative ordinances".[47] By calling them "ordinances" he implies that they are not sacraments which do something, but rites to be observed as a matter of obedience because Christ commanded them; an attitude probably a good deal more Zwinglian than Zwingli ever was! By describing them on the level of the Jewish sacrifices and priesthood which (as the Letter to the Hebrews argues) were of no permanent value, he goes on to underline this theme: "I count them not the fundamentals of our Christianity . . . servants they are . . . I therefore declare my reverent esteem of them . . . I dare not remove them from the place God has appointed; nor ascribe unto them more than they were ordered to have."[48]

Nevertheless, an attitude of increasing casualness towards the Lord's Table developed within many of the historic Free Churches. Bunyan's deeply personal and individualistic approach became quite common. "Communion Services" became increasingly separated from the main diet of worship; extra optional services to which those who wished remained after the normal exercises. It was an attitude which could easily develop from an exaggerated emphasis being put on personal assurance of salvation rather than on the corporate nature of the church. That exaggerated emphasis was almost bound to be seen when repeated periods of revival, renewal and evangelistic fervour overtook the churches. The oddly ironic result was that the type of Christian who most fervently held to the great central realities of salvation in Christ rode very loosely to that rite which most clearly proclaimed those realities.

f — The Counter-Reformation

Alarmed by the trenchant criticisms of the Reformers and by widespread defections from its ranks, the Roman Church, in 1546, summoned the Council of Trent, to restate Catholic doctrine, to remove abuse, to restore the purity of the liturgy and to set in motion the Counter-Reformation, when large areas of Europe were retrieved from the advances of Protestantism. The Council continued to meet, on and off, for the next fifteen or so years, its various decrees coming to define Catholic belief and practice until Vatican Two and beyond.

In its Decree on the Holy Eucharist the Council redefined Catholic belief in the Real Presence, transubstantiation and the most holy sacrifice of the mass. On the Real Presence it was asserted that "our Lord Jesus Christ, true God and true man, is contained under the appearances of sensible realities after consecration, 'truly' as opposed to 'in a sign', 'really' as opposed to 'in a figure' and 'substantially' as opposed to 'in the power of'." This sacramental presence of Christ does not contradict his existence in his "natural manner". It cannot be described in human terms, but is nonetheless possible to God. The basis of this belief is in the "proper and most obvious meaning of the gospels and of Paul".[49]

On transubstantiation the Council declared that "by the consecration of the bread and wine a change takes place of the whole substance of the bread into the substance of the body of Christ our Lord, and of the whole substance of the wine into the substance of his blood. And this conversion has suitably and properly been called transubstantiation by the holy catholic Church."[50] In making this declaration the Council members were probably aware of the Aristotelian categories in which the terms were used, yet, as with Aquinas, three hundred years previously, few ordinary people were aware of their precise meaning and continued to understand the declaration in more concrete and realistic terms.

On the sacrifice of the mass the Council declared that "in eating and drinking Christ's sacrifice is renewed and commemorated sacramentally and the fruits of that sacrifice are granted to the believer." The Council thus reasserted the propitiatory character of the mass, that is, its effectiveness in securing forgiveness and salvation. It also went on to defend its "canon" or form, masses in honour of the saints, ceremonies of Solemn Mass, the use of Latin in the mass and masses with only the celebrant communicating.[51]

Although the Council of Trent met twenty-five times between 1546 and 1563 it ended with its work incomplete. Although Catholic doctrine had been redefined the liturgy remained unreformed, so its final revision was left to the Pope. As a result papal power within the church was increased and a rigid uniformity of practice was imposed which has lasted well into the twentieth century. In 1570 the *Missale Romanus* was finally published wherein the central structure of the mass remained much as it had been before apart from considerable pruning of mediaeval additions. Congregational participation remained largely non-existent, the majority of the people engaging in extra-liturgical devotions while the mass was being said, and being summoned to watch only the most important moments by the ringing of a bell. Because of the nature of the papal decrees accompanying the publication of the Missal, liturgical development was excluded for the next three hundred years. Although many losses to the Reformation were regained, and missionary work extended by the tireless labours of the Jesuits, the Roman Catholic Church became theologically a sleeping church with major advance taking place elsewhere.

g — Conclusion

Was the Reformation worthwhile? Yes! a thousand times yes! Through the Reformation the Bible was restored to its central place in the life of the church and was given to the people in their own languages. Because everyone was encouraged to read the Bible for himself the Reformation became the cause of universal education now taken for granted, at least as an ideal, throughout the modern world. At the Reformation communion for everyone was restored to the church's central liturgical rite, the eucharist. All could now participate. All could feed on Christ in their hearts by faith with thanksgiving. And all could worship in their own tongue. No longer was religion a mysterious thing, a meaningless mumbo-jumbo performed by the priest on behalf of the people. It was intelligible, and under the power of the Holy Spirit it was real.

But the benefits of the Reformation were achieved only at enormous cost to the unity of the body of Christ. The atrocities committed by Catholics on Protestants, by Protestants on Catholics, and by different groups of Protestants on each other were a lasting disgrace to all the Christians involved. Even today, the wounds that were opened then, can still be used, as in Ulster, to justify strife and civil disorder throughout whole communities. And at the heart of the strife lay the eucharist, the sacrament of love, of peace, of forgiveness and of reconciliation. The task of the twentieth-century church is to restore that broken unity. Is it too much to hope that Christians of all traditions will yet be able to meet around the Lord's Table, to eat bread and to drink wine together in remembrance of him, forgiving each other as he forgave them, loving each other as he loved them, proclaiming his death until he comes and invites them all to sit at the table in his kingdom and worship and serve him together for ever?

CHAPTER FIVE NOTES

1 – See, for example, Roland H. Bainton, *Here I Stand!*
2 – Quoted in C. W. Dugmore, *The Mass and the English Reformers*, pp. 87, 88.
3 – Quoted in Yngve Brilioth, *Eucharistic Faith and Practice: Evangelical and Catholic*, p. 105.
4 – See Horton Davies, *Worship and Theology in England, Vol. 1, 1534–1603*, pp. 81, 82.
5 – Quoted in Yngve Brilioth, *Eucharistic Faith and Practice: Evangelical and Catholic*, p. 133.
6 – Quoted in *ibid.*, p. 99.
7 – Quoted in *ibid.*, pp. 99, 100.
8 – Quoted in Roland H. Bainton, *Here I Stand — A Life of Martin Luther*, p. 224.
9 – Quoted in *ibid.*, p. 224.
10 – Quoted in Yngve Brilioth, *Eucharistic Faith and Practice: Evangelical and Catholic*, p. 105, footnote 1.

11 – See Yngve Brilioth, *Eucharistic Faith and Practice: Evangelical and Catholic*, pp. 161, 162.
12 – See G. R. Potter, *Zwingli*, p. 328.
13 – Gregory Dix, *Dixit Cranmer et non Timuit*, in Cambridge Quarterly Review, CXLV 290 (1948), pp. 150, 167, 176, quoted in Kenneth W. Stevenson, *Gregory Dix — Twenty-Five Years On*, p. 32.
14 – Ulrich Zwingli, *Fidei Ratio*, quoted in G. R. Potter, *Zwingli*, pp. 337, 338.
15 – J. T. McNeill, *The History and Character of Calvinism*, p. 229.
16 – John Calvin, *Institutes of the Christian Religion*, Book IV, chapter 17, paragraph 22.
17 – *ibid.*, paragraph 29.
18 – *ibid.*, paragraph 1.
19 – *ibid.*, paragraph 5.
20 – *ibid.*
21 – *ibid.*, paragraphs 10, 12.
22 – *ibid.*, paragraph 39.
23 – *ibid.*, paragraph 43.
24 – See Gregory Dix, *The Shape of the Liturgy*, ch. 16.
25 – See Horton Davies, *Worship and Theology in England*, Vol. 1, pp. 111–123.
26 – See C. W. Dugmore, *The Mass and the English Reformers*, *passim*.
27 – Thomas Cranmer, *True and Catholic Doctrine and Use of the Sacrament of the Lord's Supper*, p. 163.
28 – *ibid.*, pp. 20, 21.
29 – *ibid.*, quoted in Colin Buchanan, *What Did Cranmer Think He Was Doing?* p. 5.
30 – See C. W. Dugmore, *Eucharistic Doctrine in England from Hooker to Waterland*.
31 – Thomas Cranmer, *op. cit.*, p. 235.
32 – *ibid.*, pp. 235, 236.
33 – *ibid.*, p. 244
34 – Gregory Dix, *The Shape of the Liturgy*, p. 672
35 – Quoted in Horton Davies, *Worship and Theology in England*, Vol. 1, p. 207.
36 – Paul Cook, *The Church*, in *Anglican and Puritan Thinking*, p. 22.
37 – Stephen Mayor, *The Lord's Supper in Early English Dissent*, p. 31.
38 – *ibid.*, p. 36.
39 – ed. Leland Carlson, *The Writings of Henry Barrow*, p. 313.
40 – Stephen Mayor, *op. cit.*, p. 37
41 – Full details in *ibid.*, pp. 141–145.
42 – John Owen, *Discourse Concerning Liturgies and Their Imposition. Works of John Owen* (chapter 7), Vol. 15, Banner of Truth.

43 – John Owen, *Discourse of the Work of the Holy Spirit in Prayer*, Vol. 4. p. 239.
44 – Para 72 of The Last Confession of John Smyth — quoted in *The Lord's Supper — A Baptist Statement* — page 14.
45 – *ibid.*, p. 15.
46 – ed. George Offer, *The Works of John Bunyan*, Vol. 3, p. 239.
47 – *ibid.*, Vol. 2, p. 604.
48 – *ibid.*, Vol. 2, p. 606.
49 – See Joseph M. Powers, *Eucharistic Theology*, p. 34f.
50 – See *ibid.*, p. 37.
51 – See *ibid.*, p. 42.

CHAPTER 6 — EVANGELICALS, TRACTARIANS AND PLYMOUTH BRETHREN

Two hundred years after the Acts of Supremacy had established the English Church, that same Church of England languished in a sad state of decadence and decay. Tired of the religious controversies which had marked the sixteenth and seventeenth centuries, the leaders of the church had settled for an easy Deism in theology and an easy rationalism in morality, both of which denied the supernatural dimension so fundamental to the Christian faith. Along with slackness in belief went abuse in practice. Plurality of livings among incumbents with consequent absenteeism was rife. Worship, such as it was, was often left to ill-paid curates, waiting impatiently for the rich pickings which would later come their way. Hundreds of church buildings were literally falling down through decay while the requirements of the Prayer Book were equally neglected. Evening Prayer had almost fallen out of use altogether and Holy Communion was celebrated no more than four times a year. Chancels, being rarely required, were used for storage, and many clergy wore nothing more distinctive than a tattered black gown, not from strongly-held theological principles, but simply because nothing else, not even a surplice, was available. Congregations were sparse, except in a few fashionable churches, where pews were owned as property, and jealously guarded by their well-heeled occupants. In such places the poor had to sit or stand at the back or in the aisles. Nor was the situation any better in the dissenting chapels. There the struggles for liberty and toleration which had characterised the seventeenth century had been largely forgotten along with Christian orthodoxy itself; Unitarianism was the prevailing theological doctrine of the day!

a — The Evangelical Revival

Yet if the general picture of English Christianity in 1730 was bleak in the extreme, two events had but lately occurred, both totally isolated from each other, which, in the course of time, would produce one of the most outstanding revivals of Christianity ever to be seen, a revival which would have a profound effect, not only on England and the United Kingdom, but also on large areas of the rest of the world. Both events were intimately connected with the eucharist.

The first event had occurred in Germany in 1727 when the Holy Spirit had fallen on a group of Moravian Christians as they had held a communion service together. The Moravians were the descendants of the Bohemian Brethren, the followers of the Czech reformer Jan Hus[1] who had gone underground when the Roman Church had attempted to suppress them three hundred years before. Now their hearts were set on fire with new love and faith as they received the bread and wine. Spontaneously embracing one another in tears, the Moravians pledged themselves to a great mission of world evangelism supported by a ceaseless vigil of prayer. For a hundred years the chain of prayer in the German community was never broken night nor day while countless numbers of others carried the Gospel to the West Indies, Greenland, North America, Labrador, Persia, Egypt, South Africa, West Africa, India and Ceylon without any guarantee of financial support beyond the all-sufficiency of God.

The second event had followed two years later at Oxford University. "In November 1729, four young gentlemen of Oxford, Mr John Wesley, Fellow of Lincoln, Mr Charles Wesley, Student of Christ Church, Mr Morgan, Commoner of Christ Church, and Mr Kirkham of Merton College, began to spend some evenings in a week together in reading chiefly the Greek Testament."[2] Such associations, or clubs, for esoteric purposes were common in Oxford at the time, and little notice was taken of the infant group until the seriousness of their religious pursuits began to earn a variety of derisive nicknames of which one, Methodists, would stick to the present day.

To the original four others were added to the Club, one of whom, John Clayton, son of a Manchester bookseller, led the members in a new direction. In his father's shop he had read many of the Fathers and constantly illuminated the group's discussions with references from the same. Soon the group had eagerly embraced the Patristic practice of weekly eucharists, celebrating them with genuflections and vestments more usually associated with the Tractarian movement of the following century.

At first sight the two events could not have seemed more distant. The "Moravian Pentecost" produced joy, love, devotion to Christ and a zeal for evangelism. The formation of the Oxford Holy Club led its members into a joyless round of religious duties, morbid confessions and awesome eucharists. And although John Wesley would soon attempt to take the Gospel to the North American Indians, his mission would fail and he would return home a broken and disillusioned man. However, the voyage to America would bring the two events together. For on Wesley's ship were a group of Moravian missionaries, and when a severe storm threatened the lives of passengers and crew alike, the Moravians alone remained calm and composed, joyfully singing and praying to God. Wesley wondered at the source of their peace and maintained his contact with the Moravians on his return to London. As a result the Patristic scholar and high-church clergyman of the Church of England entered into his own "Pentecost". On 24 May 1738, "in the evening, I went very unwillingly to a society in Aldersgate Street, where one was reading Luther's Preface to the Epistle to the Romans. About a quarter before nine, while he was describing the change which God works in the heart through faith in Christ, I felt my heart strangely warmed. I felt I did trust in Christ, Christ alone, for salvation, and an assurance was given me that He had taken away my sins, even mine, and saved me from the law of sin and death."[3] Moravian revival and Patristic rediscovery were now united in the lives of John Wesley and George Whitefield, another member of the Holy Club who had already entered, quite independently, into his own experience of salvation.

The result was not just evangelistic enterprise, social reform, the renewal of the established and the dissenting churches and the emergence of Methodism as a separate Protestant tradition. The evangelical revival quickly became a sacramental revival as well. Hundreds of eager converts crowded into their once near-empty parish churches to receive communion, often to the consternation of the mumbling incumbent, unused to such excess of enthusiasm. Where the clergy became evangelical they were quick to restore, first monthly, and then weekly communion services, as well as additional celebrations early in the morning so that industrial workers could feed on Christ by faith before the day began. In addition to all this John Wesley himself and his brother Charles worked out a unique blend of evangelical experience, a Protestant understanding of justification by faith and a Catholic understanding of the meaning and significance of the eucharist, a blend which might well point the way to reconciliation in the universal church at the end of the twentieth century.

The Wesleys' position was most ably expressed in Charles' hymns, always produced in close consultation with his brother. Here, all the elements of their creed appear in lofty, poetic language which lifts the soul from earth to heaven.

> Victim divine, Thy grace we claim,
>   While thus Thy precious death we show;
> Once offered up, a spotless Lamb,
>   In Thy great temple here below,
> Thou didst for all mankind atone,
> And standest now before the throne.
>
> Thou standest in the holy place,
>   As now for guilty sinners slain:
> The blood of sprinkling speaks, and prays,
>   All prevalent for helpless man;
> Thy blood is still our ransom found,
> And speaks salvation all around.
>
> We need not now go up to heaven,
>   To bring the long-sought Saviour down;
> Thou art to all already given,
>   Thou dost ev'n now Thy banquet crown:
> To every faithful soul appear,
> And show Thy real presence here.[4]

Here are linked, as nowhere else, the one complete sacrifice of Calvary, the offering up of the worshippers' memorial, and the continuing work of Christ in heaven as high priest. Elsewhere, the concept of eucharistic sacrifice is more strongly asserted and Charles finds no difficulty with the idea that the presentation of the bread and wine in the eucharist induces God to be gracious:

> With solemn faith we offer up
> And spread before Thy glorious eyes
> That only ground of all our hope,
> That precious bleeding sacrifice,
> Which brings thy grace on sinners down,
> And perfects all our souls in one.[5]

And again,

> .we beneath
>   Present our Saviour's death,
> Do as Jesus bids us do,
>   Signify His flesh and blood,
> Him in a memorial show,
>   Offer up the Lamb to God.[6]

From the Fathers, the Wesleys never lost their appreciation of the place and work of the Holy Spirit in transforming the bread and wine, not however into the physical body and blood of Christ, but into channels of God's love, to renew and fill their hearts:

> Come, Holy Ghost, Thine influence shed,
>   And realise the sign;
> Thy life infuse into the bread,
>   Thy power into the wine.

> Effectual let the tokens prove
>   And made, by heavenly art,
> Fit channels to convey Thy love
>   To every faithful heart.[7]

It was all a remarkable achievement. But if the Wesleys were outstandingly successful in winning hundreds of thousands of their countrymen to a living faith in Christ, they failed, for the most part, to infect them with their enthusiasm for the eucharist. Because they remained staunch and loyal clergymen of the Church of England, firmly believing in the Apostolic Succession, to the end of their days, they refused, almost to the end, to allow their local preachers to conduct communion services, advising them instead, along with their societies, to receive at the parish church. There, they were often shunned and discouraged, and the eucharist never became, for most Methodists, the joyous feast described in Charles' hymns. After the Wesleys died, confusion reigned over who could, or should, preside at the sacrament, and, in the end, most Methodists settled, in fact, if not in words, for a Presbyterian or a Zwinglian position. Indeed, many went further and drifted into a very casual approach to communion altogether. Nevertheless, "there is only one point at which an evangelical and Protestant doctrine of the Eucharistic Sacrifice has been richly expounded with true Catholicity, and which points forward, not backward, to the enriched eucharistic life of the 'coming great Church' and that is in the sacramental hymns of Charles Wesley."[8]

The Evangelical Revival was born in a communion service and resulted, among other things, in renewed eucharistic faith and practice. So what went wrong? For out of the Evangelical movement was born the Tractarian movement with controversy and bitterness which is still felt to the present day.

From its beginnings in Aldersgate Street experience was paramount to the movement, to the extent that Evangelicals laid themselves open to the taunt that they had substituted justification by experience for justification by faith. The earliest Evangelicals seemed able to sustain their experience throughout their lives, but their successors became increasingly unable to follow their example. Thus the great truths on which the movement had been founded tended to become increasingly empty shibboleths, while the high ethical and moral standards so enthusiastically embraced in the beginning tended to degenerate into a dour and joyless legalism. In such a situation it was inevitable that

Christians should concern themselves more with the form of their faith than with its exuberant expression, and the study of the Fathers, which had always been a hallmark of the Evangelicals, should result more in imitation of their ritual rather than in rediscovery of their teaching of the relationship of God and man finding ongoing expression in the eucharist.

b — *The Tractarian Movement*

By the 1830s Evangelical Christianity had reached its high watermark in the Church of England. In 1833, William Wilberforce, the great social reformer and liberator of the slaves, had died, while Charles Simeon was nearing the end of his fifty-year-long ministry in Cambridge, a ministry which had begun amid fierce opposition, but which had produced hundreds, if not thousands, of Evangelical clergy from the students of the university city. The English nation itself was in turmoil. In 1829, under threat of civil war in Ireland, Parliament had finally passed the Catholic Emancipation Act. The following three years saw unprecedented civil disorder throughout the country as working people revolted against the miseries and injustices brought about by the industrial revolution and the exodus from the land. A reluctant House of Lords was presented with the First Reform Bill, and only rejected it on the votes of the bishops; an action hardly calculated to endear the Established Church to the groaning masses. Pressure for disestablishment was growing from the dissenters (Presbyterians, Baptists and Congregationalists) who had long suffered mean and vindictive restrictions on account of their position. In 1833, the newly-elected Whig government abolished ten Irish bishoprics. To those who loved the comprehensiveness and the surpreme influence of the national church, its whole life and structure seemed to be threatened.

To three Oxford dons, Hurrell Froude, John Henry Newman and John Keble, the answer to the threat seemed obvious. If the church were disestablished, or if it had to resist the interference of increasingly hostile and meddlesome governments, then it must rediscover its authority in its apostolic succession and in its catholic heritage. To

Newman, the doctrine of the apostolic succession was explicitly set forth in the Ordination Service whereat every bishop, priest and deacon in the Church of England had been commissioned. To be sure, the Protestant temper of the age had meant that few of them had been aware of what was happening when they had received the episcopal laying-on-of-hands at their ordination. Was it not time, with the church in danger, that they should be awakened to the true nature of the ministry and position?

Thus again, in 1833, Newman anonymously wrote, had published and distributed the first of what would become ninety *Tracts for the Times* in which he pointed to the doctrine of the apostolic succession in the Ordination Service and argued its importance in establishing the church against popery, on the one hand, and dissenting preachers, on the other.[9] The Tract did not arouse immediate controversy, as is commonly supposed. Neither did the early Tracts sell very well, to the printer's displeasure, who refused further publication. Indeed, for a few years, Newman was increasingly pessimistic about the way things were going. But others joined the group, foremost of whom was E. B. Pusey, the Tracts became longer and more like treatises, and sales and influence began to increase.

Newman and Keble had been brought up as Evangelicals. Together with Froude they became keen students of the Fathers. Increasingly, the Patristic Age seemed to them to have been the most glorious in the church's history. Then, there had been but one visible church, independent of the State, drawing its strength from its apostolic succession. A conscious attempt began to racapture some of the glory of that age. Some of the Tracts advocated catholic practices such as fasting. Writings of the Fathers were published in translation. Finally, in 1841, Newman wrote and published what became the last of the Tracts, *Tract XC*, in which he argued, in a curious, legalistic way, that the Thirty-Nine Articles of the Church of England, although commonly supposed to propagate Protestant doctrine, had been framed in such a way, as not to exclude catholics from the Church of England. Indeed, any catholic could happily subscribe to them.[10]

Tract XC caused an immediate furore. Hardly anyone in England at the time, apart from the Tractarians themselves, understood that the word "catholic" could be used in any way not synonymous with "Roman Catholic". *Tract XC* confirmed the worst fears many had of the Tractarians; they were Roman Catholics in disguise, bent on destroying the Reformation and returning the Church of England to the Roman fold. Oxford University, then regarded as guardian of the church, was thrown into utter confusion as to what should be done. In the event, nothing was done except that Newman promised his bishop that no more Tracts would be published.

As it happened, *Tract XC* marked a personal crisis for Newman himself. He and other Tractarians were becoming increasingly uneasy over the assertion, that whatever they thought of the Fathers and the catholic church, there could not be two catholic churches, the Church of England and the Church of Rome. *Tract XC* marked Newman's final attempt to justify what he saw as his increasingly untenable position within the Church of England. Its hostile reception probably hastened his decision to leave. On 9 October 1845, Newman was received into the Roman Catholic Church.

A true picture of the motives of the early Tractarians is not easy to gain. From the beginning, they were seen by some as arch-plotters, planning to overturn the Reformation and to restore the authority of the Bishop of Rome within the United Kingdom. Newman's eventual conversion to Rome seemed to confirm that, and his elevation to cardinal was regarded as papal reward for his fifth-columnist activities. It is certainly true that the friends had consultations in Rome with Monsignor (afterwards Cardinal) Wiseman before they began their Oxford campaign.[11] It is certain that Froude, in particular, had a contempt bordering on hatred for the leaders of the Reformation. "The only good thing I know of Cranmer is that he burned well," he once wrote.[12]

Others regard the Tractarians as the saviours of the nineteenth-century church, delivering it from the narrow confines of its restrictive Protestantism and widening its comprehensiveness to enable it to remain a truly national church. Others again see them simply as earnest and sometimes confused enthusiasts, struggling to preserve religious values in a frightening and changing age. They had a hopeful vision of a church in which the best elements of Christian history could be combined. They were fascinated by the Fathers of the early centuries and intoxicated by mediaeval rituals and customs dimly viewed through romantic mists.

Newman's departure to Rome might well have spelled the end of the Tractarian Movement. From its beginnings, in Oxford, it had been a movement aimed at re-calling the church to a true understanding of its position before God and the State. Few practical changes had been implemented by its leaders. They remained punctilious in conducting services according to the *Book of Common Prayer*, while Newman, for example, continued to preach in a Genevan preaching gown, because this was customary in the Church of England at that time. "The writers of the Tracts always deprecated . . . any revival of disused vestments."[13] "Newman consecrated to the last at the North end."[14]

In 1839, however, the Cambridge Camden Society was founded by an undergraduate, John Mason Neale. This marked the start of the second phase of the Tractarian Movement. The leaders of the first phase had been mainly concerned to assert the apostolic succession of the bishops of the Church of England, and thus to establish the church's true catholicity. In the second phase, the service of Holy Communion was catapulted into the heart of the controversy. How it should be performed, the postures, positions and vestments its ministers should adopt, the furnishing of churches in relation to it: these were the issues raised by the Cambridge Camden Society and its associated journal, *The Ecclesiologist*.

An early publication exhorted, "Let us endeavour to restore everywhere amongst us the Daily Prayers, and (at the least) weekly Communion; the proper Eucharistic vestments, lighted and vested altars, the ancient tones of Prayer and Praise, frequent Offertories, the meet celebration of Fasts and Festivals (all of which and much more of a kindred nature is required by the ecclesiastical statutes) . . ."[15] Support for the new ideas gained ground rapidly with an increasing number of bishops encouraging change. So great, however, was the latent fear of popery among the people, that even the introduction of the surplice aroused angry mobs, while changes in the celebration of the eucharist, with candles, censing, wafers, the eastward position of the priest in relation to the altar and vestments, provoked further scenes of civil disorder. To the minds of many the issue was clear. The Mass and the Communion were two entirely different ceremonies. The Mass was Roman and hence illegal in the Church of England, which was Reformed. Contrary to common opinion, however, Evangelicals were not prominent in organising opposition to the early ritualistic changes. Only when they themselves were attacked for clinging to the old ways, did they find it necessary to organise their defence, and in time, to attempt to prevent further changes in the courts.[16]

Controversy came to a head in the 1860s and 1870s over the question of eucharistic vestments. Since the new Anglo-Catholics saw the priest as one specially ordained to consecrate and administer the sacrament, and since it had become common about the sixth century for priests to wear vestments, it was important that the priest should be seen to be a priest by wearing mass vestments at the eucharist. Since the Evangelicals regarded the priest more as a presbyter or elder than as a mediating priest, and since they believed positively in "the priesthood of all believers" it was important that the priest should not wear distinctive eucharistic vestments (which had been abandoned at the Reformation), but only the same garments he wore at other times in his ministry. By the 1860s, many Evangelicals were wearing the surplice in the pulpit instead of changing into the preaching gown, but beyond this they were not prepared to go.

Attempts to settle the ritualistic controversy in the courts proved to be counter-productive, as the imprisonment of offending clergy only gave widespread publicity to their cause and evoked sympathy for their plight. Legal judgments settled nothing; nor was the issue really settled a century later by the Vesture of Ministers Measure of 1964 which allowed the wearing of eucharistic vestments, or the surplice and scarf, "without intending any doctrinal significance thereby". If no doctrinal significance attaches to the wearing of ministerial robes, why wear them at all? Better to revert to the earliest recorded Patristic practice of "the best and cleanest ordinary garments".[17]

By the end of the nineteenth century, on practical points the Tractarians had won hands down and the Evangelicals had accepted defeat by adopting many of their reforms. Thus church buildings had been restored with chancel and altar-rail steps, interiors had been cleaned and redecorated, box-pews had been replaced by open forms, organs had become universal, choirs wore surplices, worship had become more reverent, weekly eucharists had everywhere been restored and all clergy had taken to wearing clerical collars at all times.

Alongside these practical changes, doctrinal controversy had raged as well. Although the very earliest Tractarians had promised to introduce nothing new into the Church of England, their followers soon found themselves re-examining Catholic teaching, particularly with regard to the eucharist. In particular, the writings of E. B. Pusey, culminating in *The Real Presence*, set the course of Anglo-Catholic theology for many years. Pusey accepted an objective presence of Christ in the eucharist, insisting that what is placed in the mouth is the body and blood of Christ. It followed therefore that the faithless and the faithful, the wicked and the good receive the body and blood of Christ. Pusey also insisted that the eucharistic sacrifice is no mere commemorative offering, nor the mere offering of the worshippers, their prayers and their alms, but a presentation and pleading to the Father by the priest of the same body which was broken for mankind and the same blood which was shed. Also, because Christ is present under the form of bread and wine, he is to be adored under that form.[18]

Again, as with practical reforms, although these doctrines were stoutly resisted by the Evangelicals, the end of the century saw them approaching Catholic concepts in their own teaching, and thus moving away from the nonconformists. Speaking at a conference at Fulham Palace in 1900, Bishop Moule of Durham could say, "I believe that if our eyes . . . were opened to the unseen, we should indeed behold our Lord present at our communions. There and then, assuredly if anywhere and at any time, He remembers His promise, 'Where two or three are gathered together in my name, there am I in the midst.' Such special presence, the promised evangelical presence, is perfectly mysterious in mode, but absolutely true in fact, no creation of our imagination or emotion, but an object of our faith. I believe that our Lord, so present, not on the Holy Table, but at it, would be seen Himself in our presence to bless the bread and wine for a holy use, and to distribute them to His disciples ... I believe that we should worship Him, thus present in the midst of us in His living grace, with unspeakable reverence, thanksgiving, joy and love. We should receive the bread and wine with a profound sense of their sacredness as given by Him in physical assurance of our part, as believers in Him, and so as members of Him, in all the benefits of His passion."[19]

c — The Plymouth Brethren

While Keble and Newman were struggling to restore the Catholic tradition in the Church of England, some of that church's clergy were setting their course in a different direction. In that same year of 1833, the year that Wilberforce died, the year that saw the publication of the first of the *Tracts for the Times*, John Nelson Darby, godson of Lord Nelson, made his final break with the national church and thereby catapulted Brethrenism on to the religious scene.

Born the same year as Pusey, and destined to live the same length of time, Darby was an intense young Irishman with his countrymen's love of a fight. Preparing for ordination he was "a very exact Churchman, practising what is now called Puseyism."[20] However, a period of evangelistic revival in Ireland (known at the time as the Second Reformation) was bringing large numbers of Roman Catholics into the Anglican fold. Under its influence the young curate developed clear Calvinistic views and came to believe that this church's vagueness of doctrine would prove a great source of weakness at a time of splendid opportunity.

For a while, Darby remained within the Church of England, engaging in tireless evangelistic activity throughout the length and breadth of Ireland. Gradually, however, he became disillusioned with the whole concept of a national church. Leaving the active ministry, he devoted himself to searching the pages of the Bible for a true church pattern, and to searching the churches and towns of England and Ireland for men who shared his conviction. He found them, Anthony Norris Groves, Benjamin Newton and Francis Newman whose elder brother, John Henry, was, by this time, well on the way to his cardinal's hat.

These men longed for two things, a simplicity of worship, and a freeing of the Word and the Sacraments from the binding influence of human tradition and denominational influences. Although Anglicans they soon discovered the same convictions being expressed, quite independently, by an increasing number of nonconformists. As a chemical in a liquid suddenly "precipitates" itself as a solid when the circumstances are right, so groups and individuals were coming to the surface in many places, and then gradually finding each other.

The difficulties faced by all the early Brethren centred in the eucharist. To the Anglicans, their church was too inclusive, admitting to the sacrament everyone who had been confirmed, irrespective of whether or not they had enjoyed an experience of new birth, or brought Protestant or Catholic convictions with them, or were simply being respectable and conforming to the accepted social patterns of the day. To the nonconformists, their churches were too exclusive, because they only admitted members of their particular denomination to the sacrament and refused all others. Studying the Bible together Brethren reached the conclusion "that believers meeting together as disciples of Christ were free to break bread together as their Lord had admonished them; and that, if they were guided by the practice of the apostles they would set apart every Lord's Day for thus remembering the Lord's death and obeying His personal command."[21]

So the central concept of Brethrenism emerged. All Christians are truly one. That which best expressed their one-ness is the centuries-long celebration of the Lord's Supper. It proclaims the Incarnation and atoning death of Christ. It points forward to the church's climactic hope in the return of Christ. But as it is so crucial, it must be protected from those theological speculations, priestly pretensions and denominational traditions which have made the uniting ordinance into a dividing sacrament. It was a theme to which Darby and his associates constantly returned.

"The Communion constitutes the Church; other things are only accidents,"[22] wrote Henry Borlase, one of the many Church of England clergy who threw in their lot with Darby. "The Communion Service is the outward symbol and instrument of Unity amongst God's people."[23] "The Lord's Supper is a solemn declaration to God that you regard all those who come to his table as being one with you and one with God."[24] But this was manifestly not so, particularly in the Church of England where almost anyone was free to receive communion. "It was not the *details* of the sacramental and priestly system which drove me from the Establishment," wrote Darby. "It was that I was looking for the body of Christ. It was not there."[25]

By "the body of Christ" the Brethren meant a visible expression of the unity of the church, a fulfilment of the apostle's words, "The bread which we break, is it not a participation in the body of Christ? Because there is one bread, we who are many are one body, for we all partake of the one bread" (1 Corinthians 10:16, 17).

Nor could Darby and his friends follow Newman and his friends in finding the visible unity of the church in a restoration of its Catholic ethos and succession. "Tractarianism is an advance towards Popery. To that, the principles of a true Churchman will necessarily lead if followed out to their legitimate extent."[26] Indeed, a sacramental interpretation of the eucharist was rejected completely. "I believe," wrote Darby, "that the bread remains simply and absolutely bread, and the wine, wine — that physically there is no change whatever in the elements."[27]

So far, any nonconformist would have agreed. But the argument went further. A priestly and sacrificial understanding of the sacrament is potentially divisive because it leads to the inevitable question: Who is entitled to offer the sacrifice? This problem led to that complete abandonment of the distinction between clergy and laity which has made Brethrenism so unique. The Brethren came to regard ordination as essentially a step into an exclusive priesthood, whether or not those who accepted it meant to imply that. And an ordained Methodist or Baptist minister was as unacceptable as an ordained Roman Catholic priest. As they saw it, the choice lay between a man-made priesthood and a free "ministry of the Spirit" involving the liberty of any Christian brother to preach the Word and preside at the communion within the scope of his ability and to lead worship audibly in words of his own choosing amongst his fellow-Christians. "There is no medium or resting-place for a candid enquirer between the two extremes — the ministry of the Spirit as revealed in the Word of God, or human ministry as exhibited by the ancient Church of Rome."[28]

The principle was pressed to the extreme. Church of England clergy in fairly large numbers renounced their "holy orders". Nonconformist ministers declined to receive their salaries, abandoned the title "Reverend" and either opened up the pulpits of their chapels or led a few of the congregation away to a separate gathering where "the freedom of the Spirit" could be exercised. It led to a good deal of friction. When the godly vicar of Brixham, Henry Francis Lyte, penned the immortal words of the hymn, "Abide with me", he was having problems with some of his congregation who first tried to depose him and then left his church to join the Brethren. "When other helpers fail, and comforts flee . . ." he wrote.

There was a third issue. If the question, "Who may conduct Communion?" brought the Brethren reply, "Anyone," it begged another, "Who might receive Communion?" Here, despite their early idealism and desire to break bread with all true believers in Jesus Christ, the Brethren soon found themselves giving a very different answer. For they could not admit Anglicans to their communions for they recognised Tractarians on the one hand and Scripture-denying Modernists on the other. Nor could they admit Free Churchmen for they would not recognise as Christians those who did not submit to their particular denominational identities. If anyone might administer communion, only those who joined the rapidly growing number of Brethren "assemblies" might receive it. Nor could the Brethren agree there. Darby himself used his worldwide influence to organise a close-knit fellowship of "exclusive Brethren" who were willing to follow his increasingly colourful and speculative theories which frequently conflicted with accepted Christian truth. On the eucharist, for instance, he developed the idea that the essential truth expressed therein is Christ's absence rather than his presence (for it is "until he comes"), and the certainty that Christ has died ("you proclaim the Lord's death").

The majority of Brethren, however, remained within the authentic Christian tradition, demanding "Life" rather than "light" as the only qualification for receiving the bread and wine, that is, evidence of Christian faith and character rather than doctrinal definition or sectarian affiliation. Communion is administered by unordained men with no prior arrangement as to who they should be or even at what stage in the service they should do it. There is a total lack of any liturgical formulae, and even Christ's words of institution are rarely used. There is no attempt whatever to define what is meant by the words, "This is my body." The average member of a Brethren assembly will scarcely have heard, nor will he ever use, the word "sacrament". Yet the whole atmosphere is deeply sacramental. To take part in one of these simple services at their best is to be profoundly and movingly aware of the presence of Christ, feeding on him in one's heart by faith with thanksgiving.

The Brethren never intended to form a new denomination. Denominationalism was anathema to the founders of the movement. Yet the moment "Christian brethren" left their denominational churches to "break bread" together and to meet in "assemblies" granting mutual recognition to each other, a new denomination was on the way, in fact, if not in theory. (The same process is happening again at the present time with the growth of the "House-Church Movement".) Yet the growth of the Brethren during the nineteenth century was a phenomenon of profound significance for the whole of the Western church. For the first time since the Reformation a Protestant body came into being in which the eucharist was central. Earlier chapters have shown how the principal effect of the Reformation was to exalt the Word at the expense of the Sacrament. By their example, the Brethren were the first to call a halt to this process, and to restore the equality and unity of Word and Sacrament which is the hallmark of true Christian worship.

In the strong-minded and divided Christian world of the nineteenth century, Tractarians and Plymouth Brethren seemed to be at opposite ends of the theological and ecclesiastical spectrum. In reality, they were far closer than they realised at the time. For, faced with the problems of a church at the end of the Evangelical Awakening, drifting again into formalism and social respectability, and threatened by the rising tide of destructive liberalism, both the Tractarians and the Brethren saw that the church's only hope lay in the restoration of the eucharist as the outward symbol of the unity of God's people who together formed the body of Christ in the world. Both movements drifted into formalism themselves in which empty shibboleths and human traditions assumed greater importance than the apostolic tradition which both, in their very different ways, claimed to represent.

Newman, Pusey and Keble would never have believed that the restoration of Catholicism would fail to restore the glory and influence of the national church. Neither could they have conceived that in the mid-twentieth century the Roman Church would abandon the Tridentine Mass, modify its sacrificial understanding of the eucharist, and be willing to call its priests presidents. Equally, Darby and Groves would have met with incredulity the assertion that Christ would not return in their lifetime, that a vast new Christendom would arise in Africa, Asia and South America, and that the old structures of "corrupt Christendom" would experience several periods of revival, renewal and reformation. Nevertheless, between them, they helped to lay the foundations of the twentieth-century church in which the understanding and practice of the eucharist has become increasingly important.

EVANGELICALS, TRACTARIANS AND PLYMOUTH BRETHREN

CHAPTER SIX NOTES

1 – See above, p. 83f.
2 – John Wesley, *A Short History of Methodism*, quoted in G. R. Balleine, *A History of the Evangelical Party in the Church of England*, pp. 2, 3.
3 – John Wesley, *Journal*, 24 May 1738.
4 – *The Methodist Hymn Book*, number 771.
5 – Quoted in J. Ernest Rattenbury, *The Evangelical Doctrine of Charles Wesley's Hymns*, p. 225.
6 – Quoted in *ibid.*, p. 225.
7 – *The Methodist Hymn Book*, number 767.
8 – E. Gordon Rupp, article in *The Manchester Guardian*, 6 April 1955.
9 – *Tract I*. Quoted in A. O. J. Cockshutt, *Religious Controversies of the Nineteenth Century*, pp. 63–66.
10 – See selections from *Tract XC*, quoted in A. O. J. Cockshutt, *Religious Controversies of the Nineteenth Century*, pp. 74–90.
11 – *Protestant Dictionary* article on *Oxford Movement*.
12 – Quoted in E. J. Poole-Connor, *Evangelicalism in England*, p. 215.
13 – E. B. Pusey, letter to Bishop Tait, quoted in G. R. Balleine, *A History of the Evangelical Party in the Church of England*, p. 180.
14 – E. B. Pusey, letter to Scott, quoted in Balleine, *ibid.*
15 – See Horton Davies, *Worship and Theology in England*, Vol. 3, p. 272.
16 – See G. R. Balleine, *A History of the Evangelical Party in the Church of England*, pp. 172–184, especially p. 173.
17 – See above, p. 52.
18 – See W. H. Mackean, *The Eucharistic Doctrine of the Oxford Movement*, p. 122.
19 – Quoted in Yngve Brilioth, *Eucharistic Faith and Practice: Evangelical and Catholic*. p. 219.
20 – *Collected Writings of J. N. Darby*, Vol. 1, p. 56.
21 – E. M. Broadbent, *The Pilgrim Church*, p. 347.
22 – Quoted in H. H. Rowdon, *Origins of the Brethren*, p. 272.
23 – H. Borlase, *The Present State of the Church*, p. 12.
24 – Quoted in H. H. Rowdon, *op. cit.*, p. 239.
25 – *Collected Writings of J. N. Darby*, Vol. XIV, p. 413.
26 – H. Borlase, *Christian Witness*, 1, p. 43.
27 – *Letters of J. N. Darby*, Vol. 2, 1868–79, p. 15.
28 – R. M. Beverley, quoted in H. H. Rowdon, *op. cit.*, p. 274.

CHAPTER 7 — TWENTIETH-CENTURY RENEWAL

By the beginning of the twentieth century the Christian church throughout Europe, North and South America, South Africa and Australasia appeared never to have been stronger. In country after country, in its various Catholic, Orthodox and Protestant forms, the church enjoyed a formal relationship with the State. In many other countries, even where no formal link existed, the church was a powerful influence in society. Throughout Africa and Asia thousands of missionaries were labouring to win the world for Christ within their lifetime. The time indeed seemed near when the earth would be filled with the glory of God as the waters cover the sea.

In fact, the strength of the church was far more apparent than real. Although numbers of professing Christians had increased steadily throughout the nineteenth century, the church had largely failed to keep pace with the population explosion which had accompanied the industrial revolution, so, in relation to society as a whole, the church was weaker at the end of the century than it had been at the beginning. Nor did church leaders anywhere foresee, in 1900, the effects that the Communist Revolution in Russia, two world wars and the general process of secularisation would have on the strength of their communities. By the middle of the century, in the older countries of "Christendom" the church was, in general, weaker than it had been for centuries, while in Russia and Eastern Europe it was enduring its bitterest onslaught since the days of the Roman Empire. In the face of this unprecedented decline the watchword of the twentieth-century church has become "renewal" and this, nowhere more so than in the area of eucharistic understanding and practice.

a — Liturgical Renewal in the Roman Catholic Church
In earlier pages the effects of the sixteenth-century Council of Trent on the nature and celebration of the mass in the Church of

Rome were outlined.[1] There it was noted how pre-Reformation theology was essentially restated, while liturgical reform itself was left to the Bishop of Rome. This resulted in a rigid uniformity being imposed on the church with the mass being said in Latin by the priest on behalf of the people. While he read the rite facing the altar the people occupied themselves with extra-liturgical devotions which often had little connection with the eucharist itself. At three points in the service, at the offertory, at consecration and at communion the congregation was summoned by a bell to watch what was happening at the altar and recommended to observe certain "affections". Since it was generally held that communion must be preceded by confession, and since the majority of people only confessed at Christmas, Easter and Pentecost, lay communion was rare. Even when it was received it was only in one kind (lest the blood of Christ should be spilled on the floor!) and it was dispensed, before, after or even completely apart from the eucharistic celebration itself and then, not with the host which had just been consecrated, but with the reserved sacrament from previous celebrations which was kept in a "tabernacle" at the side of the altar. Mass was thus mainly attended and observed, and communion occasionally received, for the acquisition of merit, and this idea was reinforced by the continuing practice of votive masses for specific purposes and requiem masses for those who had died.

However, during the early nineteenth century a re-awakening sense of their own history led Roman Catholics to examine the origins and meaning of their liturgical practices. Continental monasteries experimented with different forms of the mass, more frequent communion, and the participation of all who were present. Anglo-Saxon Catholics (whether in Britain or America) were suspicious, and papal approval was slow and reluctant.

However, in 1947 Pope Pius XII promised liturgical renewal and inaugurated a decade of increasing change and relaxation. By the time the famous and radical Second Vatican Council was having its effect in the early 1960s, changes little less than astonishing were sweeping away much of the old order. Today there can seem to be (at any rate on the surface) little difference between a Roman Catholic mass and an Anglican communion. The words are all in the vernacular, the priest (or "president") stands behind the altar facing the people, the congregation is fully involved, lay people assist in important parts of the service, the public reading of Scripture is prominent, ceremonial vestments and decoration are greatly simplified, communion is received regularly and increasingly, both bread and wine are served. Startled onlookers have witnessed what seems to be a Protestantising of the whole thing, although the changes have not gone quite as far as that.

Moreover, the changes have not been only in form. They have arisen from changing theological concepts. There is a new appreciation of the church as a community, as the body of Christ (rather than as a hierarchy). This is the reason for the changing status of the laity and the encouragement of Bible-reading which have produced such a striking *volte-face* on the part of a church which once boasted that it never changed and which struggled to keep the Bible out of the hands of its people.

How significant is the actual re-statement of Catholic eucharistic *theology* which has accompanied this liturgical renewal? The "Real Presence" is now rarely defined in the old terms of transubstantiation which cost so many Catholics and Protestants their lives in an earlier century. *Trans-signification* is the current expression. The really significant factor is seen as the action of the Holy Spirit in the whole eucharistic prayer rather than in the priest's words of consecration. Thus the *epiclesis*, or prayer to the Holy Spirit, has reappeared in the new prayers. Moreover *Sacrifice* is no longer defined in terms of repetition, but in terms of *re-presentation*. The sacrifice of Christ was offered once-for-all in history on the cross (another startlingly Protestant phrase!) and its re-presentation at each eucharist is seen as recalling before God and before man, his saving acts in Christ, thus making them effective again to the believing community.

This is not exactly vintage evangelicalism, but it is certainly a far cry from the hard and rigid salvation-by-sacramental-manipulation so characteristic of Pre- and Post-Reformation Catholicism. Suitably emboldened by these changes, some Protestant scholars have gently suggested that Rome might travel further. There has often lurked in Catholic thinking a tendency to look on the mass as a commemorative meal. As priest and people gather around the altar which is their common table, the Lord is remembered in the special situation of his death, and the bread and wine present that death in symbol.[2]

b — Liturgical renewal in the Anglican Community

(i) The Prayer Book Debate

By the beginning of the twentieth century the Church of England was deeply divided between Catholics and Evangelicals, with a third group, the Broad Church party, attracted by liberalism and the social gospel, uneasily holding the middle ground. Anglo-Catholic "innovations", in particular the use of the Canon, or form, of the mass, and reservation of the sacrament after communion for adoration, flourished unchecked despite Evangelical opposition backed by legal judgments and penalties imposed by the State. The reassertion of the Catholic tradition in the Church of England had been born out of fear of State intervention in church affairs, and the Anglo-Catholics were thus increasingly irritated by what they regarded as the attempts of a secular state to control religious beliefs and practices. Finally, in an attempt to bring peace out of strife and order out of chaos, a Royal Commission on Ecclesiastical Discipline was appointed in 1904 and reported in 1906. It concluded that "the law of public worship in the Church of England is too narrow for the religious life of the present generation. It needlessly condemns much which a great section of Church people, including many of her most devoted members, value."[3]

"Letters of Business" (a legal and ecclesiastical device) were accordingly issued to open the way for the first revisions of the Prayer Book in two and a half centuries. The tortuous events which finally resulted in their rejection by Parliament in 1927 and 1928 need not be recalled here. They look curiously dated fifty years later when it would be difficult indeed to imagine modern Members of Parliament becoming agitated about how a Christian should pray. Suffice to say that the two major stumbling-blocks were provision for reserving the sacrament, and the suggestion of a eucharistic prayer which included an *epiclesis*.

Evangelical joy at the preservation of the 1662 Prayer Book which they viewed as a guardian of Protestantism, was short-lived. Bishops soon made it clear that technically illegal use of the new liturgies would be viewed with something less than disapproval. Events were soon to develop in any case.

(ii) The Shape of the Liturgy

On the second Sunday in Advent, 1927, the ancient church of St John in Newcastle-upon-Tyne added further to its colourful history (it was handed over to the Baptists during Cromwell's Commonwealth!) by inaugurating a parish eucharist. It was the beginning of the parish communion movement which spread rapidly, first among Anglo-Catholics and later among all types of Anglicans. The idea combined many of the insights gained by both Anglican and Catholic examination of the historical roots of the eucharist. Prominent amongst them was an Anglican monk from Nashdom Abbey in north London, Dom Gregory Dix. He persistently maintained that the Fathers rather than Cranmer gave expression to the church as the Body of Christ. After the Second World War, Dix published his *magnum opus*, *The Shape of the Liturgy*. This vast, rambling, but eminently readable work has aroused strong passions, but its influence has been profound. Anglican (and non-conformist) worship in the 1980s and beyond will be the better, or the worse, for it.

In *The Shape*, Dix asserted that from the very beginning of the Patristic period the original shape of the Last Supper, as recorded in the Gospels, had been transformed into the shape of the eucharist proper, a shape it held inviolate, despite many additions, to the time of the Reformation. According to Dix, the action of the Last Supper was sevenfold: Christ took bread (1), blessed it (2), broke and shared it (3), ate the meal with his disciples (4), took the cup (5), blessed it (6) and shared it (7). By the second century this sevenfold action had become fourfold: (1) offertory (i.e. the bringing of the bread and wine to the table by the worshippers and the offering of the bread and the cup in the eucharistic prayer), (2) thanksgiving (i.e. the prayer of thanksgiving over the bread and wine including repetition of Christ's words of institution at the Last Supper), (3) fraction (i.e. the breaking of the bread) and (4) communion. According to Dix the eucharist should therefore conform to this shape and not the shape of the Book of Common Prayer.

The idea, that, in the Patristic period, the eucharist was a sacrifice and that the sacrifice came to consist in the offering of the bread and wine to God as the body and blood of Christ, has been outlined in chapter four. But to Dix, the offering of the bread and wine took place not only during the eucharistic prayer when the words "we offer to thee this bread and this cup" were recited. It also occurred earlier in the service when the worshippers solemnly placed their own gifts of bread and wine on the communion table. For Dix this was not merely a utilitarian act whereby, at a time of great danger when it was illegal to celebrate the eucharist, Christians supplied their own elements for the solemn meal and thus spared their brave host in whose home the meal was eaten from being detected in the course of its preparation. For Dix the placing of the bread and wine on the table was a deeply ritual act wherein the fruits of the earth were solemnly offered to God as symbols of the people's lives and labours, offered that they might be transformed and used in his service. For Dix, the germ of this offertory, and therefore its justification, lay in Christ's taking of the bread and wine, prior to giving thanks over them at the Last Supper.

During the 1950s Dix's theory resulted in the development of increasingly elaborate offertory processions in which the bread and wine were carried in great pomp to the altar in many Catholic churches, of England. It was therefore all the more surprising when the first real criticism of Dix came from this same Catholic tradition where he enjoyed greatest support. In a lecture on *The Paris Communion*, Michael Ramsey, then Bishop of Durham, later Archbishop of Canterbury, declared:

> The new movement [i.e. the parish communion movement] places too much emphasis upon the offertory, as the offering to Almighty God of the bread and wine as the token of the giving to him of the people's common life. Appropriate ceremonial brings out this moment in the rite; layfolk carry the elements in procession from the back of the church, and lumps of coal and other objects may be brought to the church to reinforce the point. And this point is indeed a true and Christian one, for though its place in the New Testament is a little obscure it finds vivid expression in St Irenaeus (e.g. *Adv. Haer.* xvii. 5; xviii. 1). The idea of sacrifice is taught in many parishes in connection with the offering of bread and wine in the offertory, and ourselves, our souls and bodies, in the prayer after the Communion.
>
> By itself, however, this sort of teaching about sacrifice can be a shallow and romantic sort of Pelagianism . . . For we cannot, and we dare not, offer aught of our own apart from the one sacrifice of the Lamb of God.[4]

If Dix's offertory theology was suspect, maybe its premises were also at fault. In 1971, in *Jesus Said Grace*, B. A. Mastin argued that Jesus' taking of the bread and wine at the Last Supper was merely preparatory to and integrally part of his act of giving thanks, or saying grace over them.[5] If Mastin is right, then this action of Jesus had nothing like the significance attached to it by Dix.

More recently still, Colin Buchanan has insisted that although Christians did take their own bread and wine to communion services during the second and third centuries, their action was purely functional and not ritual, as Dix suggested. Indeed, Buchanan has trenchantly accused Dix of deliberately distorting the Patristic evidence to support his theory, and has urged that the time has come to bring the offertory to an end in Anglican eucharists.[6]

However, despite all Dix's faults, *The Shape of the Liturgy* was probably the greatest piece of liturgical writing in the twentieth century. In it Dix directed the attention of Catholics in the Church of England away from the Church of Rome (which many had been satisfied to ape) to the spirituality and practice of the early Patristic period, and thus to a lively appreciation of the church of the body of Christ with every member having his part to play in the church's worship. Evangelicals might say that Dix did not look back far enough, and that he should have concentrated his efforts more on the apostolic than the Patristic period. In view of this, Evangelical reluctance to relinquish Morning and Evening Prayer in favour of Holy Communion as the central service of the Sunday is surprising, to say the least. Some are coming slowly to the new pattern, but for many the primacy of word over sacrament (when they should really be complementary), and an unwillingness to recognise anything of value in "Catholic" practices remain all too important.

(iii) The Alternative Services

The Prayer Book debacle of 1928, despite the later semi-legalisation of the "Deposited Book" set back the cause of liturgical reform in the Church of England for many years. It also demonstrated the folly of attempting to introduce new forms of worship by Act of Parliament without giving church people the opportunity to test them in practice for an experimental period beforehand. Elsewhere in the Anglican Communion, in Scotland, the United States and South Africa, in Ireland and Canada, where the churches were unfettered by the restraints of State law, liturgical revision proceeded more cautiously, yet more successfully, throughout the early years of the twentieth century. When the Church of England came to tackle the issue again it had the example of many of its daughter provinces to follow to avoid the kind of embarrassing controversy which had done so much damage in the earlier years of the century.

In 1966 Parliament passed the Prayer Book (Alternative and Other Services) Measure and allowed new services to be introduced provisionally in addition to those of the 1662 Prayer Book. Series One was the immediate result. In effect this finally legalised the 1928 material with the exception of the alternative eucharistic prayer which had caused so much trouble in the first place. In Series Two bitter controversy was aroused over the proposed inclusion in the eucharistic prayer of the phrase "we offer unto thee this bread and this cup" and the offending phrase was subsequently deleted. Series Three departed from all archaisms in language. The Alternative Service Book of 1980 incorporates most of the new material together with four alternative eucharistic prayers and a modernised form of the 1662 Communion Service. Thus, it is hoped, all traditions from Catholic to Evangelical have been provided for, along with opportunity to introduce variety into a hitherto rigidly controlled service. Fears have been expressed that different churches will settle on one or two of the eucharistic prayers according to their churchmanship, and to allay these fears the compilers have felt it necessary to express the hope that all the prayers will be widely used at the minister's discretion.

All the new eucharistic material since Series One is modelled on Dix's fourfold "shape". Provision for reservation of the sacrament after a communion service and an *epiclesis* are also included. Explicit mention of the "once for all" nature of Christ's sacrifice is sometimes made, while provision for the omission of manual acts during the eucharistic prayer reflects the view that the whole prayer effects consecration rather than the repetition of Christ's words themselves at the Last Supper. Thus, the new eucharistic material in the Church of England is now modelled on Biblical and Patristic theology, unlike the Prayer Book which is Biblical and reformed. It thus reflects the change in emphasis from Protestant to Catholic which has characterised the church during the twentieth century.

Elsewhere in the Anglican Communion many more new rites have been introduced. All reflect the influence of Dix, but they vary in their theological emphases according to the "Protestant" or "Catholic" character of the provinces concerned.[7] The Methodist Church has also produced a similar rite, *The Methodist Sunday Service*.

(c) *Liturgical Movements in the Free Churches*

Sometimes because of clearly-understood conviction and sometimes because of mere tradition and prejudice, the non-Anglican and non-Lutheran churches of Protestantism have held aloof from any precise and detailed liturgy, and this has of course affected their celebration of communion. Presbyterianism has usually distinguished between Common Prayer (which it rejects) and Common Order (which it accepts with varying degrees of enthusiasm). In other words, it favours a general outline of worship which follows a Biblical pattern, but does not employ compulsory forms of words for the congregation to use. Congregationalists and Baptists have gone further and have been inclined to suspect "*form*" at all.

A kind of race-memory of struggles against a legally-enforced Prayer Book has combined with half-recognised cultural factors and a profound suspicion of anything which interferes with "worship in spirit and in truth". The witness which the Free Churches have borne to what is truly essential in genuine and acceptable worship has always been necessary, and always will be. To them, discussion of "validity" in terms of the correct formula, the correct order of events, the correctly qualified "priest", etc, etc, are utterly meaningless. They see in such discussions a tendency to deny the free grace of God, the spiritual nature of worship, the completeness of Christ's work of reconciliation and the priesthood of all believers.

Added to this cheerful disregard of liturgical niceties, has been a less healthy neglect of the eucharist itself. Though all orthodox dissenters pay lip-service to the importance of the Lord's Supper, their practice often belies this. The historical accident of the sixteenth century's Genevan civil authorities' refusal to allow Calvin a weekly celebration of communion has become a precedent never intended by that Reformer. Communion has often become an optional extra (often offered at odd and arbitrary intervals; such as every quarter, or the third Sunday morning of every month). The Liturgy of the Word has been disastrously separated from the Liturgy of the Upper Room.

It is this realisation which has come to increasing numbers of thinkers and leaders in the Presbyterian, Congregational and Baptist churches of the world (as well as to the more Anglican-inclined Methodists who, as has been seen, have their own strong historical precedent). A Liturgical Movement (parallel with those already described amongst Catholics and Anglicans) has developed among the dissenters. The value at least of Common Order has been recognised, and most denominations have published service-books and manuals which draw on the riches of earlier devotion throughout Christendom. The communion service is being restored to its proper place. "It is a departure from apostolic worship to celebrate the Lord's Supper infrequently, or to regard it as a brief appendage following another complete service. Christian worship is essentially eucharistic," says the preface to a Baptist order-book.

The four-fold shape advocated by Dix has been quite widely accepted in a modified form. Raymond Abba, a Congregationalist, has written — ". . . every classic liturgy has four great actions answering to those of our Lord in the Upper Room: 'He took', 'He gave thanks', 'He brake', and 'He gave'. These, together with the Words of Institution which are their warrant, are integral parts of the sacrament, which is incomplete if any of them is omitted . . . Celebrations of the Lord's Supper which are gravely defective are all too common in many of our churches."[8]

Admittedly, the emphasis in Free Church circles is much simpler. There the stress is on the four *actions* of "taking" the bread and cup (i.e. displaying them), "giving thanks", "breaking" the bread, and "giving" to the congregation. The prayer of thanksgiving is frequently offered by lay church officers who very often instinctively follow the pattern of more liturgical thanksgivings. The actions, admittedly, are often themselves treated in a cavalier fashion. Sometimes there is no actual loaf to break and it can be known for there to be no wine in the cup. This becomes possible because of modern practices of having little pre-cut squares of bread ready for distribution and hygienic individual glasses containing anaemic fruit-juice. However, this carelessness is not an illustration of non-conformist practice but a departure from it. As the bread and wine are taken to the seated congregation there is a good deal of unconscious ceremonial which underlines the authentic Free Church insistence that it is the whole action of the Lord's Supper that gives it authenticity. "This we *do*, following the example and obeying the command of our Lord Jesus Christ, who in the very night in which He was betrayed took bread . . ." This familiar formula, never actually written out but instinctively followed by most ministers, says it all.

Dix's luxuriant development of the act of "taking" as a ceremonial offertory has found little favour in such circles. Perhaps that is significant; it is the part of his argument which rests least on clear Biblical precedent and most on Patristic example. Perhaps even that is seen in a modified form in the slightly ritualistic uncovering of the Table after the sermon, and the subsequent taking of an extra collection called the communion offering. This is usually to be spent at the discretion of the minister on special social needs within the local fellowship, and it is normally placed beside the bread and wine on the Table, with implications of which the particular congregation may or may not be aware.

What the Liturgical Movement in Free Church circles has done is to raise the fundamental question, "What is liturgy *for*?" Those who are used to liturgy as a fact of religious life rarely stop to ask so fundamental a question. They have no need to; it is there and (they may feel) needs some revision. But *why* is it there? When thinkers from a church tradition which can do quite happily without it (or thinks it can), begin to examine it, they go further back. That is what non-conformists have begun to do, and their contribution is important, because it shifts the centre of some of the intransigent historical arguments to a different place.

The Baptist Stephen Winward, for example, has argued powerfully that Christian worship must be understood in terms of giving to God as well as receiving. British worshippers have slipped into coming to church to "get a blessing" rather than to "make an offering", he says chidingly. There is no difficulty in showing how unbiblical *that* is. Moreover, Christian worship is incarnational, and therefore bound to have sacramental overtones. In other words, God's revelation was in flesh — in a living, active Man. The Christian's response should therefore embrace the whole of his manhood; his actions and senses as well as his thoughts and words. Looking at the

Incarnation, it can hardly be doubted that the visible and material matter!

He goes on to argue that Christian worship is communal. If all of God's people are to be involved in declaration and response, then liturgy in some form is inevitable. But its purpose is to provide precisely that communal exercise, not to impose a form of words in some way assumed to be valid.[9] Its validity, if the word must be used, is found in the fact that it truly reflects the communal experience and Biblical conviction of the worshippers.

This leads to the vital principle underlined by all non-conformists when they take sacraments seriously. They see the essential importance of the sacrament to lie neither in the elements used (what happens to the bread? is it changed?) nor in the words employed (what is the formula? which words are essential?) but in the whole dramatic combination of Word of God and responding actions of man. P. T. Forsyth has written, "The exact point of the Lord's Supper is that *such symbolism did not lie in the elements but in the action*, the entire action — word and deed . . . It was the *action* that was symbolical, the breaking rather than the bread, the outpouring rather than the wine."[10]

This is classic Protestantism (even if Protestantism's most consistent descendants, the Free Churches, have sometimes forgotten it in their dislike of "ritual"). Because man's redemption was accomplished through the death and resurrection of Christ, it is *his redeeming work* which gives their meaning to the Gospel Sacraments. Thus they consist essentially of *action*, and as Forsyth says, "their action is symbolic of Christ's Act, not of His essence."[11]

d — The Ecumenical Movement

The missionary movement of the nineteenth century highlighted the futility and stupidity of exporting Western denominational differences to the countries of the European empires and their spheres of influence. From the start many missionary societies agreed not to work in each other's areas, with the result that, to the present day, different parts of Africa, Asia and Central and South America are predominantly Anglican, Baptist, Methodist or whatever in their Christian communities. The twentieth century, however, has seen the remarkable growth of the ecumenical movement as Christians around the world have awoken to the scandal of their disunity and have worked to heal the divisions caused by earlier historical situations.

Initially, the ecumenical movement represented efforts among Protestants to work more closely together, with the formation of the World Council of Churches, in 1945, marking a more definite commitment towards ultimate unity than had been achieved hitherto. Now the World Council numbers among its members Russian and Eastern Orthodox churches, and a growing number of Pentecostal churches. The WCC represents a high level of commitment towards unity: at local level groups of churches in towns and villages have come to work more closely together than ever before in witness, worship and fellowship.

Inevitably, there have been very varied reactions to the Ecumenical Movement, and ironically it has caused as much division as unity. During its purely Protestant stage its leadership has often been in the hands of the more liberal theologians and many evangelicals have kept aloof from an organisation which (to judge by its official statements) had little interest in preserving Biblical beliefs. The suspicion has been unavoidable at times that theology was either kept in the background for the sake of chumminess, or given curious new forms that would have astonished earlier generations of Christians. It has not been difficult at times to caricature the movement as a ship with no name, manned by a crew who all speak different languages, and who will agree at some later stage of the voyage who the captain is and what the destination is. Since the addition of Eastern Orthodoxy to the ecumenical ranks and the growing relationship with Rome, many Evangelical fears have been further deepened. They see as almost axiomatic a growing monolithic structure greatly weighted in favour of Catholic thinking, with a grim inevitability about the answer to the question, "Who will eventually run it?" The answer is, "The Pope, of course." So evangelicals themselves have become divided between those who are "In it to win it" and those whose slogan is, "Come out from among them."

In spite of all this, an ecumenical *climate* (not necessarily the same thing as the World Council of Churches) has done nothing but good in its demand for Christians to sit down together and listen to each other instead of sniping at each other from entrenched positions. Often the result is a surprised and delighted discovery of essential one-ness. That in turn raises the problem of intercommunion. The refusal of some Christians to admit other Christians to their fellowship at the Lord's table must rank as the greatest scandal of disunity, and the ecumenical movement has forced Christians of all traditions and denominations to examine their practice in this respect. Practice varies enormously from some of the Baptists who maintain an "open table" inviting "all who love the Lord Jesus" to share in every communion, to others like the Roman Catholics who restrict communion to those who have been baptised and confirmed in their own church.

Actual practice often varies from official policy. Until quite recently no Church of England clergyman was supposed to admit to communion any who were not baptised and confirmed in that church. In practice, visitors were never turned away, nor were questions ever asked of occasional communicants. The present policy of admitting to occasional communion those "in good standing" with their own churches, not only recognises current practice but breathes a more charitable attitude towards visitors from other denominations, while attempting to retain some semblance of discipline.

Among Protestant Christians, evangelicals have always led the way in their practice of inter-communion. Their many interdenominational conferences and conventions have often included communion services using many different rites in which all have shared irrespective of their particular allegiance. Sometimes these services have been held out of an instinctive desire to realise the ideal of "all one in Christ Jesus" without any determined attempt to recognise and resolve differences in belief and practice. To this extent discussions at national and international ecumenical levels have avoided the realisation of vague and undefined "unity" and have done much to increase understanding and decrease suspicion between different churches and traditions.

The ecumenical atmosphere has produced more than a mere friendly getting-together. Genuine dialogue between members of different traditions has developed (whether at official denominational level, or between prominent individuals). The ill-fated attempt to reconcile the Church of England and the Methodist Church eventually came to grief on the verge of achievement. It could be argued that what destroyed it was the inability of sufficient Anglicans to be able to say that Methodist ministers are true priests in the apostolic succession. The old problem of validity in ministry and sacrament had proved to be insoluble once more, and the sad story recorded in this book received further illustration.

A short-lived excitement was caused when, through their disappointment at this outcome, two Anglican Evangelicals (C. O. Buchanan and J. I. Packer) and two Anglican Catholics (E. L. Mascall and the Bishop of Willesden) had a series of private encounters which led to the publishing of *Growing into Union* in 1970. In the event, nothing came of the hopeful scheme, and the two Evangelicals lost a lot of their former friends and admirers. The book acknowledges (on behalf of all four writers) that the New Testament never speaks of the Lord's Supper in terms of sacrifice, and that the attempt to relate such terms to the New Testament is artificial. But it goes on to say, "Yet we are a Christian priesthood in our corporate unity, and there is surely a sacrifice of some sort we are to offer as priests?"[12] What is it that we offer, then? The document increasingly takes on the form that theologians so dearly love; the qualifications and half-definitions which leave the layman more confused at the end than at the beginning:

> Not mere bread and wine . . . not merely the fruit of our lips; not merely undefined spiritual sacrifices; not merely ourselves considered apart from Christ, not even ourselves in Christ, if that is seen in separation from our feeding on Christ; but ourselves as re-appreciated by Christ.[13]

> . . . our self-offering as responsive to God's grace, which is contemporaneous with the reception of the remediated salvation.[14]

What does that mean? Is it simply the Reformation view that the believer replies to God's grace in a life of gratitude? If so, why is it so insistently linked with eucharistic offering and sacrifice? And if it means only that, how can Dr Mascall write elsewhere?

> In the Eucharist the earthly Church is given a share in the continual offering which the glorified Christ perpetually makes before the Father's throne in heaven.[15]

Until 1960 the Roman Catholic Church remained officially aloof from ecumenical advances. The Second Vatican Council, however, gave way to the pressure for a changed attitude by that church to the "separated brethren". Increasing contacts have been made between Roman Catholics and Orthodox and Protestant churches in the years that have followed. In particular, the visit of Archbishop Ramsey of Canterbury to Pope Paul VI in Rome in 1966 resulted a year later in the setting up of an Anglican-Roman Catholic Joint Preparatory Commission, which, in turn, resulted in the appointment of the Anglican-Roman Catholic International Commission (ARCIC) in 1969. Two years later the *Agreed Statement on Eucharistic Doctrine* was published, indicating the areas of understanding on which the two teams of delegates were agreed.

The remarkable success of ARCIC in publishing the *Agreed Statement* after four hundred years of distrust, suspicion and separation between the two churches was due, in no small measure, to the rapport which was quickly established between two of the delegates to the Commission, Revd Julian Charley, then Vice-Principal of St John's College, Nottingham, and Revd Fr Jean M. R. Tillard, Professor of Dogmatic Theology in the Dominican Faculty of Theology, Ottawa. Both delegates presented papers to the Commission for discussion, and both wrote the *Agreed Statement* between them at St John's College prior to the Commission's meeting at Windsor in 1971 which resulted in its publication.

Fr Tillard has since published the paper he wrote for discussion by the Commission.[16] Particularly in its treatment of the eucharistic sacrifice and the mode of the Real Presence, this paper demonstrates how Roman Catholic dogma can be presented in a form (on the surface and for some distance under the surface) much more acceptable to Protestants. The *Agreed Statement* shows the fruit of such thinking.

On *The Eucharist and the Sacrifice of Christ*, it is stated,

> Christ's redeeming death and resurrection took place once and for all in history. Christ's death . . . was the one, perfect and sufficient sacrifice for the sins of the world. There can be no repetition of or addition to what was then accomplished once for all by Christ. Any attempt to express a nexus between the sacrifice of Christ and the eucharist must not obscure this fundamental fact of the Christian faith.[17]

The report then suggests a way ahead in the more recent understanding of remembrance in the Passover celebration.

On *The Presence of Christ*, it is stated,

> Communion with Christ in the eucharist presupposes his true presence, effectually signified by the bread and wine which, in this mystery, become his body and blood.[18]

An intriguing footnote adds,

> The word *transubstantiation* is commonly used in the Roman Catholic Church to indicate that God acting in the eucharist effects a change in the inner reality of the elements. The term should be seen as affirming the *fact* of Christ's presence and of the mysterious and radical change which takes place. In contemporary Roman Catholic theology it is not understood as explaining how the change takes place.[19]

The report goes on,

> Christ is present and active, in various ways, in the entire eucharistic celebration. It is the same Lord who through the proclaimed word invites his people to his table, who through his minister presides at that table, and who gives himself sacramentally in the body and blood of his paschal sacrifice. It is the Lord present at the right hand of the Father, and therefore transcending the sacramental order, who thus offers to his church, in the eucharistic signs, the special gift of himself. The sacramental body and blood of the Saviour are present as an offering to the believer awaiting his welcome. When this offering is met by faith, a lifegiving encounter results . . . we must recognise both the sacramental sign of Christ's presence and the personal relationship between Christ and the faithful which arises from that presence.[20]

Finally, the report records that traditionally the consecratory prayer is "a word of faith addressed to the Father" and that "through this prayer . . . the bread and wine become the body and blood of Christ by the action of the Holy Spirit, so that in communion we eat the flesh of Christ and drink his blood."

Needless to say, Protestants will be coughing by the time they read these last words, if not before. However, it is a very remarkable document. Unless it is going to be claimed that the leadership of the Roman Catholic Church is engaged in a gigantic plot to hoodwink Protestants (a kind of worldwide ecclesiastical Watergate) then it must be acknowledged that their thinking is undergoing very considerable change. Significantly, however, the *Agreed Statement* bears only the authority of the International Commission and, thus far, it has not been endorsed by either church. More recently, Lord Coggan, when Archbishop of Canterbury, has called for immediate intercommunion between Roman Catholics and Anglicans and, while his call has been officially refused, significant numbers of both churches are receiving communion together on various occasions. Eucharistic differences would now seem to centre more on the problem of ecclesiastical authority than on doctrinal understanding.

e — The Charismatic Movement

Perhaps the most remarkable feature of twentieth-century Christianity worldwide has been the rise and growth of Pentecostalism. Early in the century Christians in different parts of the world discovered and began to exercise supernatural spiritual gifts, particularly speaking with tongues and healing. Separate Pentecostal churches were quickly established and have since enjoyed remarkable growth, particularly in Latin America. After that initial phase the movement was largely ignored by the older western Protestant churches.

Around 1960 Christians in mainline Protestant churches again began to rediscover supernatural Pentecostal gifts and the modern "charismatic movement" was born. Unlike the earlier movement, however, this movement has largely remained inside the established churches and, with the exception of the "house-church movement", further division has been avoided. Neither has the movement remained exclusively Protestant. Particularly in the United States large numbers of Roman Catholics have been affected by the movement and have made a distinctive contribution to it.

The doctrinal emphasis of the charismatic movement is the Holy Spirit who, through baptism in the Spirit, brings the Christian into a living conscious relationship with Christ. The fruits of the Spirit are then displayed in transformed characters, and the gifts of the Spirit are bestowed for Christian service and the strengthening of the church which is the body of Christ. The movement has stressed the interdependence of Christians in the church and the need for all Christians, through exercise of their various gifts, to play a full part in the church's ministry. In this respect the charismatic movement has complemented the liturgical movement which has also emphasised the idea of the church as the body of Christ and the need for all its members to play their proper part in the celebration of the eucharist.

This is the most likely explanation of a curious fact. The movement in its first wave (classic Pentecostalism) was an expression of American frontier-fundamentalism: second-blessing orientated and totally non-liturgical, even anti-liturgical. Yet in its second wave (Charismatic Renewal) it has been widely accepted in Anglican and Roman Catholic circles and has become a friend of liturgy and eucharist. It did not leap upon churches which were previously static, but presented itself to churches where there was already a seed-bed of concern for liturgical renewal and the better expression of the church as the Body of Christ. It provided the energy for which liturgists were looking.

Meanwhile, amongst non-conformists, the charismatic element has often led to a better understanding of liturgy and an increased emphasis on communion. Less cerebral and word-dominated than most Free Church worship, charismatic worship is emotional, spontaneous, immediate, and seeks expression in action and gesture and posture. With their hand-clasps, upraised arms in prayer, linked hands, swaying and dancing, they have reminded Protestants that,

> none of us can park our bodies at a meter outside of worship and go disembodied into worship . . . To them worship includes celebrating their own incarnate state![21]

This is of major importance, especially when it happens to non-conformists. For what is then seen is *liturgy and sacramentalism in the making*. On the surface, charismatic spontaneous ceremonial and Catholic fixed ceremonial seem to be poles apart; the first is done in immediacy because it has not been done before, whereas the second is done in tradition because it has always been that shape. But already the spontaneous is becoming the accepted (almost the *expected*: one would have to be very brave and free *not* to sing with uplifted hands in some churches!). What is happening is new liturgy taking shape in a living situation — as the old did, and presumably for similar reasons. It raises vital issues. Is the "validity" of a liturgy or sacrament to be seen, not in its formulae or in its actions, but in the living presence of the Holy Spirit who moves worshippers to speak and to act?

This is seen when charismatics approach the eucharist. From the beginning of the movement, the many conferences held to promote its aims have found their climax in a celebration of the Lord's Supper. In the atmosphere of such a gathering, the living presence of the Holy Spirit in worship-encounter is seen as the central key to communion as to all other renewal activities. It is he who makes Christ real to the assembled gathering. Therefore the invocation of the Holy Spirit on the elements of bread and wine and on the assembled people is seen (and very much *felt* . . . always the mark of the charismatic) to be much more important than the repetition of the right formula or the valid ordination of the presiding leader (often leaders, plural; an Anglican, a non-conformist and, if at all possible, a Roman Catholic jointly presiding).

For this reason, charismatics have welcomed with particular delight the restoration of the *epiclesis* in the newer liturgies. It seems to them to be truly providential that Series 3 Communion and Charismatic Renewal have arrived at the same time.

> No-one seemed to realise the awe-inspiring importance of the invocation of the Holy Spirit in the anaphora until the fresh springtime of the Churches which we call the charismatic renewal. The liturgical movement had prepared the way for this as far as charismatic worship is concerned. In the Church of England Series 3 we pray: "Grant that by the power of your Spirit, these gifts of bread and wine may be to us his body and his blood," and "Renew us by your Spirit, inspire us with your love, and unite us in the body of your Son, Jesus Christ our Lord." So when charismatics go to the eucharist nowadays where the new rites are used, these words vibrate with relevance. Having a greater openness to the Holy Spirit in their own lives, and being newly aware of the presence of Christ through his activity in the Christian fellowship and in the spiritual gifts, the epiclesis enables them to respond to God in praise and thanksgiving in ways that were unimaginable before. Indeed, what we call baptism in the Holy Spirit is basically a personal epiclesis which is renewed in the liturgy. This is one of the reasons why the new rites make

such excellent vehicles for the "extended eucharist" that we encounter in charismatic gatherings. It is as if the Holy Spirit has been preparing the Churches, through the work of their liturgists, for just such a celebration . . . what matters is what God works by the power of the Holy Spirit through the sacramental signs, not our attempts to define what we should do or say when we celebrate the Lord's Supper . . . We do not, I believe, have to wait until we can discern what are "valid orders" in those who preside over eucharistic celebrations. What we have to obey is the prompting of the Holy Spirit and the orderliness which he reveals . . . That is why the epiclesis has been rediscovered by Christians of different Churches in such a vital way. It cuts across our denominational barriers as a sword-like word from God, and it reflects profoundly our increasing faith by the Spirit God really is fulfilling his promises.[22]

These are words whose significance has yet to be fully explored. As the first enthusiasm of the Charismatic Renewal calms down and an era of respectability and acceptance begins, its most permanent contribution to the worldwide church may be a break-through of understanding in this area.

CHAPTER SEVEN NOTES

1 – See above, p. 118f.
2 – See E. J. Koenker, *The Liturgical Renaissance in the Roman Catholic Church*, p. 115.
3 – *Report on Ecclesiastical Discipline*, pp. 75, 76, quoted in G. J. Cuming, *A History of Anglican Liturgy*, pp. 211, 212.
4 – A. M. Ramsey in "The Parish Communion" in *Durham Essays and Addresses*, p. 18.
5 – B. A. Mastin, *Jesus Said Grace*, Scottish Journal of Theology, Vol. 24, No. 4, February 1971, pp. 449–456.
6 – See Colin Buchanan, *The End of the Offertory — An Anglican Study*, passim.
7 – See C. O. Buchanan, *Modern Anglican Liturgies*.

8 – *Principles of Christian Worship (With special reference to the Free Churches)* by Raymond Abba, Oxford University Press, 1957.
9 – Winward argues this in detail in Chapter 1 of *The Reformation of our Worship*.
10 – *"The Church and the Sacraments"* P. T. Forsyth, p. 234.
11 – ibid p. 243.
12 – *"Growing into Union,"* C. O. Buchanan *et al.*, p. 100 and p. 59.
13 – *ibid.*, p. 59.
14 – *ibid.*, p. 60.
15 – *All in Each Place*, edited by J. I. Packer, p. 167.
16 – See J. M. R. Tillard, *Roman Catholics and Anglicans: The Eucharist*, in *One in Christ*, July 1973.
17 – *The Three Agreed Statements* CTS/SPK 1978, p. 9.
18 – *ibid.*, p. 10.
19 – *ibid.*, p. 10.
20 – *ibid.*, p. 11.
21 – *Encountering Charismatic Worship*. Grove Booket No. 51. Colin Buchanan. p. 17.
22 – *Theological Renewal* October 1978, pp. 30–32.

CHAPTER 8 — CURRENT ISSUES

The road from the Last Supper in the Upper Room on the night when Jesus was betrayed to modern eucharistic faith and practice in the Christian church has been long, tortuous and diverse. Along it, Christians have been persecuted by the State and by each other. Sometimes they have worshipped in joyful assurance of their Lord's presence and in confident expectation of his triumphant return. Sometimes Christ's presence in the sacrament has been hidden and distorted by magic and superstition. Sometimes, great Christians have struggled with lofty words to explain and lay hold of the sublime truths conveyed in the celebration of the Lord's Supper. Often Christian understanding has been partial and shallow. After centuries of neglect many Protestant Christians are rediscovering the importance and centrality of the eucharist in worship. After centuries of suspicion many Catholics and Protestants are feeling the urge to break bread together again, and to heal the rifts which have divided them for so long. What then are the crucial issues on which Christian differences remain? Are they capable of solution?

To some Christians, agreement is clearly impossible, and the search for such agreement is itself open to suspicion. Writing in response to the document *Growing into Union* (see page 157 of this book) an Evangelical commented,

> The hope of a final rapprochement between Catholics and Protestants is kept alive by the belief that somehow, somewhere, a new ground of synthesis and agreement will be found which has been overlooked by controversialists of the past. The fact is that every square inch of the ground has already been covered, indeed was covered before the Reformation was fifty years old, by the most able Protestant and Catholic theologians. There is simply no place to stand where another has not already stood;

excepting of course the fence, and it would appear that it is this which our authors have succeeded in mounting.[1]

This attitude is understandable. But is it really true that every possible area of common ground has been explored, every conceivable argument exhausted? Must it be said that because revered spiritual forefathers gave their immense minds to the problem without success (and did so in the context of a depth of spiritual conviction and experience that shames Christians today), that it is smacking of the impious or the arrogant to suggest that it be looked at again? For surely some things *have* changed. The position of one of the parties has changed. It is a simple fact (as has been shown) that some modern Catholics (whether Anglican or Roman) now hold a position identifiably different from that of the Council of Trent which virtually closed discussion at the end of the Reformation. It is a simple fact that some thoughtful and influential Catholics will now dismiss "transubstantiation" as a mediaeval attempt to explain the mystery of the eucharist, couched in phrases and reflecting forms of thought which are no longer applicable (if they ever were). To a Protestant, this may not be nearly enough, but it introduces a genuinely new element. If one of the parties in a seemingly intractable controversy shifts his ground quite perceptibly, then there *is* something new to explore and something new to say.

There are other new factors, too. By *modern historical methods*, it is now possible to understand the gradual development of liturgy over the centuries. The contenders during the Reformation were not able to do this. They attacked or defended the great liturgies and ceremonies *as they then existed*, with little reference to how they had got that way. To say that, is not to denigrate the Reformers any more than it would be to point out that they did not understand the Law of Gravity.

A further new factor is the *modern understanding of the wholeness of man*. Modern medicine unites with Bible teaching to present human nature as an integral unity, *not* a soul inside a body but distinct from it, nor a being with spiritual needs divorced from physical and mental needs. The modern word *psychosomatic* exemplifies that rediscovery. Some insights of psychology also illuminate the vital connection between what a man *does* and what he really is in the depths of his being. Surely this can be helpful in looking again at the whole concept of the sacramental.

Underlining this is another important fact. *Traditionally non-liturgical branches of the church* are looking at sacrament and rite with a new friendliness. Because they do not take the old arguments for granted, they are able to see things in a refreshingly new light. They are saying things which used not to be said.

Furthermore, the striking phenomenon of the Charismatic Movement has brought a new dimension to the discussion. It is hard to find their insights expressed by either side in those old arguments which covered every square inch of ground before the Reformation was fifty years old.

Are there, then, areas of understanding?

a — *Ordinance or Sacrament*

Here is one of the fundamental questions, though be it noted that there are evangelicals on both sides. Is the Lord's Supper an ordinance only? In other words, is the feast celebrated quite simply, because Christ commanded it? Is the direction of its action from man to God, in the sense that it is a declaration of faith in what God has done? Or is a sacrament being celebrated; a means of grace in which the life of God is made effective towards man?

Neither of the technical words is strictly Biblical. And surely the two concepts do not have to be exclusive of each other. Clearly the command is obeyed, "Do this . . ." and obviously in doing it "the Lord's death is proclaimed . . ." and all that is believed about it. That is what is meant by ordinance. But equally clearly the words of Christ in John 6 and the teaching of Paul in I Corinthians 10, point to a vital relationship between observation and blessing received. The cup of blessing is a "participation in the blood of Christ". To eat and drink in an unworthy manner is to profane the Lord's body and blood. And that is what is meant by sacrament.

Need the two concepts, then, be put in opposition? Is not an artificial dichotomy the very thing that has done the harm? Obviously the first emphasis must be on what God has done and is doing. His action is first and last: man's worship is but *antwort* to God's *wort*, as Luther insisted — an answer to his Word.[2] But that immediately presupposes that man responds to that Word in faith and obedience and worship. Without that, a Sacrament is as void and empty as a seal hanging on a parchment that has nothing written on it[3] (to quote Calvin).

So sacrament and ordinance go hand-in-hand, and a truly Biblical Christianity proclaims, not indeed a Gospel of sacraments, but sacraments of the Gospel.

b — Sacrament or Sacrifice?

Is it possible to go further and see in the Sacrament of Communion some kind of sacrifice? Here is where the going becomes very hard indeed, and feelings run high.

The eucharist is not a sacrifice in the sense that it turns away God's wrath and makes him mercifully disposed towards the worshippers in the church in which it is celebrated. Only one sacrifice ever did that; God's own sacrifice of himself in the life and death of his Son at the cross. That sacrifice was unique. It was offered once for all. It was unrepeated and is unrepeatable. During mediaeval times the eucharist was so closely identified with Christ's Passion that it came to be regarded, in the popular mind at least (and often at higher levels than that, if words mean anything), as a repetition of it every time it was celebrated, and therefore as the ongoing means of forgiveness and reconciliation. Thus the unique character of Christ's single sacrifice was compromised, and Christian devotion came to consist solely of attendance at the mass. The idea that in the eucharist God is somehow appeased, was reasserted in the sixteenth century at the Council of Trent, and despite modern welcome Roman Catholic restatements of faith, the Tridentine Decrees have never been renounced. Thus, deep differences remain between Catholic and Protestant understanding of the nature of eucharistic sacrifice.

The revival of the Catholic tradition in the Church of England in the nineteenth century led to the idea of the re-presentation of the sacrifice of Christ in the eucharist, but to many Protestants this still sounds suspiciously like repetition. The suspicion is sometimes underlined by the whole ethos which surrounds the celebration of the eucharist; candles, incense, vestments and the like. Catholics in the Church of England have also developed the idea of the eternal self-offering of Christ in heaven, and have linked this with the idea of the church as the body of Christ on earth, so that, in the eucharist, the whole Christ offers the whole Christ.[4]

To Protestant Christians, and to evangelicals in particular, this whole understanding of the eucharist continues to present very real and special problems, for they feel that it compromises the very heart of the Christian Gospel. On the basis on Christ's cry from the cross (John 19:30), and on the insistence of the writer to the Hebrews of the single, once-for-all nature of Christ's sacrifice, Evangelical Christians place strong emphasis on the finished work of Christ. For them, this is crucial, for it is the ground of their assurance of salvation. Only because Christ has offered a sufficient sacrifice for sin which is received by faith, can Christians be sure their eternal salvation is guaranteed, dependent, not on anything they might do, but on the finished work of Christ. Any eucharistic doctrine which compromises the complete sufficiency of that work will thus be suspect in evangelical eyes. The problem is so hard to define, without being uncharitable. Catholics and Evangelicals may celebrate the eucharist using identical words and identical rites, yet because they are doing different things in their celebration, division and suspicion remain.

Is there any way in which the word "sacrifice" can be applied to the eucharist, then? It quickly came to be so in the early church of the Fathers (Chapter 3) and it is easy to sympathise with the reasons whilst shrinking from the later results. The word "sacrifice" is also applied in the New Testament itself to activities as diverse as preaching the Gospel, giving money, and surrendering one's life to God (Chapter 2). Since at the eucharist the Lord's death is proclaimed, money is given, and love and obedience are offered, the word sacrifice would seem to be applicable enough, *but not in any exclusive sense*. It is only "sacrifice" in the sense that *they* are. To make some kind of verbal accommodation on that basis in order to placate Catholic demands for sacrificial language *by which they may mean something else* is dangerous and confusing. Is that what the "Agreed Statement" is doing? Is that what "Growing into Union" was doing?

> Evangelicals acknowledge that they are to present their bodies as a living sacrifice to God, their sacrifice of praise and thanksgiving, of prayer and service; and they know that these things are accepted not for any worthiness in themselves, but solely for the sake of their Saviour Christ. But at no point, however high in the scale you go, does this sacrifice merge and become identical with the sacrifice of Christ . . . The two can never be fused or synthesised conceptually without grave danger arising. Extravagant and bewildering language on this subject is therefore not helpful. However hard one tries, what an Evangelical means by sacrifice can never be made to carry the significance of what a Catholic means by sacrifice.[5]

Problems remain also in connection with the Offertory, that is the offering of the bread and wine to God as symbols of life and labour that they may be transformed for God's service and for the redemption of society. The incipient Pelagianism inherent in this view has been identified by no less a figure than Michael Ramsey himself, yet the Offertory processions continue in many Catholic eucharists. Pelagius was the father of the "British heresy" and the idea that man can somehow please God by being good and religious and respectable has persisted ever since. Man cannot please God except by receiving the benefits of the one sacrifice of Christ, and while ever eucharistic celebrations continue to compromise that truth, division will remain in the body of Christ.

The problem here is that Catholics are using a pleasant and edifying and Biblical idea (the sanctification of everything that is offered to God in Christ's name) and giving it a context *which the Bible simply nowhere implies* . . . and then go on to insist on the essential nature of this extra-Biblical addition.

c — The Real Presence — Physical or Spiritual

Christ's presence in his church is a constant New Testament theme. Christ is always with his people, to the close of the age (Matthew 28:20). Where two or three are gathered in his name, there he is in the midst of them (Matthew 18:20). How the Christian church came to associate the presence of Christ with the eucharist and how that presence came to be centred in the bread and wine has been the theme of this book. At one extreme have been those who have asserted that the bread and wine are physically transformed into the body and blood of Christ. At the other extreme have been others who have insisted that Christ is present only in the hearts of his believing people. Some have posited the Holy Spirit as the means of Christ's presence, others the repetition of Christ's words at the Last Supper, others the act of communion and others the exercise of faith.

Ever since Aquinas, some Catholic theologians have denied the physical transformation of the elements, though Protestants may feel that this has rarely been grasped by the vast majority of Catholic worshippers. Associated with an extreme objective view of the presence of Christ in the eucharist has been the much-abused practice of reservation. To take some of the bread and wine from a communion service to the absent sick has much to commend it, stressing as it does, their continuing fellowship with the church and the concern of the church for their restoration to health. But to keep some of the elements permanently reserved, to bow to them and to say prayers to them as in the Roman Catholic service of Benediction will continue to be abhorrent to Protestants. Jesus, the Lord of glory and eternal King, cannot be confined to bread and wine, nor can he be locked away in a little cupboard! Equally, Catholics are shocked by Protestant casualness in practice, particularly as found in the Free Churches. There, the serving of the wine in individual cups, the chopping of the bread into individual fragments (sometimes without a loaf to be broken), and the inattention given to the very words of institution used by our Lord, confuse and puzzle them. To them, that is not only a contradiction of the action of Christ and his disciples at the Last Supper. It is also a fundamental denial of the unity of the church and of its fellowship with its one Lord.

Yet here there is surely the opportunity to think again. Some Catholics are now at least hedging their words on transubstantiation. A priest known to one of the writers of this book (and far from being a trendy youngster) dismisses transubtantiation as a not-very-successful Aristotelian explanation of what happens, which has lost its relevance. Many Catholics are content merely to quote the words of our Lord, "This is my body", "This is my blood", and leave it at that. He certainly never said, "This turns into my body" as Catholics used to insist. But nor did he say, "This represents my body" as Protestants have often insisted.

Can it now be agreed that Christ is not physically present in the bread and wine? Christians seem to be moving somewhere near to that. Can Christians be patient with those whose loyalty to received traditions and whose struggles with *the actual words of Christ* require them still to look for some formula to express what happens? Is there some hope of a way ahead in looking again at the word *sign* which, in the Reformers' usage meant a great deal more than it does in modern English (a mere symbol)? When the combination of Word with sacrament is required is there not a hopeful path to better understanding? The sacrament does not in itself add anything to the Word, any more than the kiss and the ring at a marriage service add anything to plighted troth. But surely the reiteration within the use of kiss and ring give effect to the vows made. So the sacraments "be certain sure witnesses and effectual signs of grace . . . by which He doth work invisibly in us, and doth not only quicken but also strengthen our faith in Him" as the Thirty Nine Articles declare.

Can modern psychology help here, too? The principle taught by psychologists, that inner attitudes are strengthened and developed by outward bodily expression, has an important bearing on the devotional life. Indeed, more can be said than this. For when devotion is absent or dormant, outward performance can often awake or evoke it. It is often assumed that actions are always the outcome of thoughts, emotions, and volitions. This is only one side of the truth. As the psychologists James and Lange have emphasised, the expressive actions of the body can also quicken and strengthen emotion. Action can also evoke emotion. Anger is increased when a man clenches his fists and strikes a blow. If he makes himself smile and bursts into laughter, he will probably begin to feel cheerful. The expressive actions of the body do react for good or ill on the human spirit. It was the denial of this truth that led Baron von Hugel to say, "What a curious psychology which allows me to kiss my child because I love it, but strictly forbids me to kiss it in order to love it."[6] "The outward performance of cultic acts, ritual and sacrament, can evoke devotion when it is dormant or strengthen it when it is already active."[7]

Are there parallels to be found in the understanding of the psychosomatic? Doctors once dismissed as folklore the idea that worry causes duodenal ulcers or stress causes heart disease. Now they know better. Thoughts and emotions and attitudes which have no actual physical existence do in fact produce physical counterparts — everything from asthma to migraine, from cancer to arthritis. The Bible implied this from the beginning, in its portrait of man as a living soul, a body-mind-spirit unity. The idea in reverse, so to speak, is implied in the embodied presence of God in the Old Testament. Solomon knew quite well that the vastness of the heavens could not "contain" God — yet the Ark of the Covenant, sign and symbol of God's presence with his people, is spoken of almost interchangeably with the presence itself. "God is gone up with a shout" (Ps. 47:5), "Arise, O Lord, and go to thy resting-place" (2 Chron. 6:41).

Often Christian devotion and instinct is able to move faster than theological definition — especially in hymns. It is amusing to see how willing extreme Protestants are to *sing* words which they would long hesitate to *say*.

> *Thy presence* makes the feast;
> Now may our spirits feel
> The glory not to be expressed,
> The joy unspeakable.

Not only followers of John Wesley sing this quite happily. And Baptists are quite cheerful about including in their hymn-books,

> Come, risen Lord, and deign to be our guest
> ... Thyself at Thine own board make manifest
> in Thine own sacrament of bread and wine.

A Congregationalist bids ...

> Behold the eternal king and priest
> ... Himself the master of the feast
> His flesh and blood the food divine.

... and Plymouth Brethren sing without a qualm,

> Thy body broken for my sake
> My bread from heaven shall be.

Are they speaking of the once-for-all act on Calvary? Or of the local Breaking of Bread? Do they know? Does it matter?

Charles Wesley dismisses the notion that the eucharist can be explained or defined.

> How He did these creatures raise
> And make this bread and wine
> Organs to convey His grace
> To this poor soul of mine;
> I cannot the way descry,
> Need not know the mystery;
> Only this I know — that I
> Was blind but now I see.

That is the authentic word of Christian testimony and devotion. God has acted in Christ. He has declared his action in his Word. His Spirit confirms it in individual experience. It is the great theme of *immediacy* which is at present so associated with Charismatic Renewal but is by no means exclusively a Pentecostal experience. Somewhere along this route, surely, the whole area of debate on Christ's presence in the eucharist with its hitherto contradictory positions may be found to be complementary. If it can be agreed that Christ is not physically present in the bread and wine, then hopefully it can be agreed that he is both objectively and subjectively present. He must be objectively present, or how could anyone who eats the bread or drinks the cup of the Lord in an unworthy manner be guilty of profaning the body and blood of the Lord? Equally, those who eat and drink, must eat and drink in faith. The Holy Spirit must be active, making Christ present in the eucharist, calling forth adoration, joy and thanksgiving from the worshipping community. The mode of Christ's presence is best left undefined; this book has attempted to show the deep waters in which Christians have been engulfed when they have tried to be too precise in attempting this definition.

d — Validity or Reality?

The last point raises acutely the whole matter of what is meant by a *valid* eucharist. A great deal of this book has been taken up with accounts of varying ceremonies and formulae. To many Protestants the whole thing (apart from the theological differences) is a matter of taste and custom and aesthetics. They wish to use appropriate and fitting words at the eucharist, and they probably notice whether the few actions involved are suitable, but it is little more than that. There is no "right place" for the Lord's Prayer to be included, no great significance in the timing of the Offertory, no anxious ascertaining that the required actions are performed when the words of institution are repeated. For their minds simply do not work that way, and their faith is not committed fundamentally to that kind of issue. But to the Catholic mind, these things are crucial. Certain phrases employed by certain people make the whole thing *valid*. If those factors are not present, it is *invalid*.

This means that the historic divide between Protestant and Catholic Christianity is ultimately about a difference in the interpretation of Christian history. A Catholic interpretation traces the history of the church back in an unbroken succession to Peter and the remainder of the apostles. Authority is vested in the church, and Scripture and the church's traditions regulate its beliefs and its life. Only eucharists celebrated by priests ordained by bishops standing in the apostolic succession are valid. Those who reject the authority of the Catholic church thus reject Christ himself. Protestants, however sincere and well-meaning, are therefore in a state of disobedience and need to return, in penitence, to the fold of the one true church.

Protestants, on the other hand, claim to find the church's authority, not in a visible organisation, but in the Word of God. According to this view, the Catholic church began to depart from the truth of God's Word early in the second century. False teaching and practice became ever more widespread until, apart from a few notable exceptions here and there, the mediaeval church became so enmeshed in unscriptural additions and superstitions as to resemble the Antichrist. From this sorry state of affairs the church was rescued by the rediscovery of the Word of God and the Reformation in the sixteenth century. That may be an over-simplification, but it roughly covers the state of affairs. And the Protestant who understands this is naturally pleased when he sees Catholics thinking again, and happy to hear that he and his fellow-worshippers are now "separated brethren" rather than "heretics" . . . but he has to ask, "Separated from *what*?" From an organisation which alone is valid, and whose sacraments alone are effectual? In that case, what in objective fact is meant by validity? The question is pressing and crucial, and it divides Protestant from Protestant, as was seen in the failure of Anglican-Methodist union. Here is the crunch. Here is the test of what is really meant by the presence of Christ, by the completeness of the atonement, by the grace of God even.

For example, one of the authors of this book is a Baptist minister. He presides at communion services in a church which combines strong evangelistic advance and modest emphases on the charismatic and the liturgical in worship. The Lord's Table is attended by large numbers of Christians (many of them recently-declared Christians) at gatherings quite often characterised by quiet fervour, deep solemnity, and a most marked sense of God's presence. Sometimes Anglican Series 3 is followed in whole or in part. Quite often an *epiclesis* is included and a Baptist common-order book is employed. Sometimes there is no formal and recognisable *epiclesis* . . . usually because its place has been taken, in the style of Calvin's Geneva, by a hymn or prayer invoking the Holy Spirit's blessing on the preached Word. Sometimes a Prayer of Thanksgiving from the minister includes conscious words of remembrance with appropriate actions but sometimes laymen "give thanks for the bread and wine" with deep sincerity, in truly Biblical language, and with murmurs of agreement from the congregation. God is clearly present by his Spirit.

Or is he? If he is not, it is difficult to know what else Christians mean by the presence of God. What then constitutes the presence of God? Is Christ present in a special way when the words of the *epiclesis* are used, but not so present when they are omitted? If there are appropriate words of remembrance, will the people feed on Christ in a manner impossible when a mere layman prays an unstructured prayer? Or is the whole service invalid anyway, since the writer, unlike his colleague, is not a member of a ministry regarded as being in the apostolic succession and marked by episcopal ordination? And if it is not valid, what do we mean by that word?

Is there, for example, less of a *subjective experience* of the joy of assurance, the word of pardon, the peace that passes understanding? Are the eyes of faith dimmed in some way, so that the worshippers do not so clearly behold God's glory? Is their giving of themselves in self-surrender and oblation any less complete?

Or is it something more objective that is lacking? Was the nature of Christ's finished work upon the cross in some way unfinished after all, unless it has added to it a valid eucharist? Does the Holy Spirit withhold the full *application* of that work, perhaps, because of some inadequacy of ministry or Sacrament?

It is at this seemingly hopeless point of collision that the Charismatic Renewal may have more to say to us than is yet realised. Many "renewed" non-conformists often develop a broader sympathy towards the whole concept of liturgy and sacrament, whilst "renewed"

Anglicans hail with delight the rediscovered *epiclesis* in the newer liturgies. What is happening? People are discovering in renewed joy and liberty the promises of the Gospel to be fulfilled within their own subjective experiences. The words become real; the concepts become dynamic; the truth takes wings. Apart from the more controversial gifts of tongues, etc, it has all happened before, in the church's time of advance and reformation. When that happens, the words become more valuable, not less; but there is an instinctive desire to incarnate the words and the experience in act and gesture and symbol, too. Liturgy develops, before the eyes. It has to, because the people of God are together and rejoice, because they are the body of Christ, because corporate worship requires by definition some shape, because Christ has redeemed them, body, soul and spirit. And it is this that makes the words and actions valid. They are true. They correspond with a recognised and felt and experienced reality.

> The Spirit answers to the blood
> And tells me I am born of God.
>
> New songs shall now my lips employ
> And leapeth my glad heart for joy.

They knew it, and sang about it, in the eighteenth-century Awakening.

So the charismatic writer already quoted in his welcome given to the epiclesis writes, "I detect a common consensus that beneath all the niceties of one eucharistic doctrine as compared with another, what matters is what God works by the power of the Holy Spirit through the sacramental signs, not our attempt to define what we should do or say when we celebrate the Lord's Supper."[8]

Certainly, this phenomenon compels Christians to look again, not so much at their bookshelves full of documented evidence of what earlier Christians said and did, but at what the grace of God is doing amongst Christians today. The writer goes on to speak of a new awareness of Christ's presence, and explains, "This experience is not based on the adoption of a high doctrine of the eucharistic presence or the eucharistic sacrifice, but on something that they feel in the deepest part of their hearts when they break bread together in a loving fellowship that expects God to speak and act in its midst."[9] Is this not what the inspired record describes when it states that the first Christians "with one mind kept up their daily attendance at the temple, and, breaking bread in private houses, shared their meals with unaffected joy" (Acts 2:46 NEB)? Is this not what the first Methodists meant when they said, "Thy presence makes the feast"?

A vivid illustration is provided by the Coptic church in Egypt and Ethiopia (all the more usefully since few English readers are likely to be irritated by the use of this example). Like all Eastern churches, the Coptic has enshrined an *epiclesis* in its eucharist. Equally enshrined (the word is particularly appropriate) is the reverence visibly paid to the Bible. It is carried into services with pomp and ceremony, often gold-covered and encrusted with precious stones — and yet unread; written in a language not used by the people. The words of the epiclesis were there. More — the very words of Scripture were there. But until recently the Coptic church was so numbed by tradition and fossilised in ceremonial that evangelical missionaries have had to regard it as an alien religion and have needed to evangelise its members. Now the scene has changed. A wave of renewal has come to the ancient church. "The Spirit of God is today moving in many Coptic churches. There is a movement of truly born-again youth. Numbering in thousands, they are fearlessly evangelistic. There are numerous born-again Coptic priests who are filled with the Holy Spirit. Pentecost is outpoured in copious measure in several of the ancient cathedrals."[10]

What, in view of this, constituted the "validity" of this church's sacraments? Surely only the sovereign presence of a gracious God whose voice has long been muted and whose Spirit has long been grieved (but who has not been guilty of that at times?) now livingly revealed again.

Of course there is an obvious danger in this suggested approach. Charismatic experience (or any other kind) can easily become a new Gnosticism, in which the criterion of God's presence is thought to be mystical experience or feeling rather than the promise of his Word believed and acted on. It is possible to leap out of the frying-pan of Galatian heresy (God's grace restricted to legal ceremonies) into the fire of Corinthian heresy (God's grace measured by exotic experience). "In Christ dwells all the fullness of the godhead bodily, and ye are complete in Him," is still the guiding principle (Colossians 2:9). That completeness is found, not in either the right formulae invoked or the right feeling evoked, but in his gracious presence and in man's believing response to him.

e — Grace or Achievement?

One of the truths to which men must constantly be recalled is the truth that God works in free and sovereign grace. Nothing could be more fundamental to the New Testament revelation. All that God has done in Christ was done because he chose to save those who deserved nothing but judgment. "For by grace you have been saved through faith; and this is not your own doing, it is the gift of God — not because of works, lest any man should boast" (Ephesians 2:8, 9). Every genuine work of spiritual renewal in the church's history has re-emphasised that truth; it is bound to be so, for the Holy Spirit cannot contradict himself. For if God acts according to grace at all, then it must be by grace alone: man cannot and must not seek to add to what he offers in unconditional freedom. But if salvation is granted by grace alone, it must be received by faith alone. Men and women can only reach out empty hands and freely receive it. That is the meaning of faith, and if anything is added to that faith, then it is not grace alone that saves. This means that neither self-produced morality nor the observance of religion however scrupulous, can effect salvation. To establish this, the apostle Paul fought the Galatian heresy tooth and nail. At that time the sacramental effort which was being promoted as a necessary aid to salvation was circumcision. "If justification were through the law, then Christ died to no purpose" (Galatians 2:21). "If you receive circumcision, Christ will be of no advantage to you" (Galatians 5:2). The same applies to any other ceremony, however sacred. After all, did not God himself ordain circumcision? But further, if salvation is through faith alone, man can only believe it to be so, and find assurance in that belief, because God has declared it. God's Word in Christ, attested by apostles and prophets, and finding ongoing expression in the fellowship of his church can be the only ground of man's faith (see Ephesians 2:19, 20).

Now if any Biblical understanding of the eucharist is to be found which will reconcile or bring closer the differing approaches, it must be shaped by these three great principles.

(i) A true eucharist must express the grace of God

If the eucharist is to unite and not to divide Christians it must avoid any emphases which might compromise this fundamental truth. In the past, not only has the Catholic concept of "merit" effected such a compromise; so has the Protestant concept of "worth". Merit is not credited to the Christian because he attends or watches the eucharist, or because he receives the bread and wine. The Christian's only merit is in Christ, and his only righteousness comes through faith in Christ's finished work. Nor should the Christian avoid the eucharist because he is unworthy. Of course he is unworthy. Only Christ is worthy, and the Christian comes to the eucharist, to rejoice again in the total, free forgiveness effected in the work of Christ and to receive again the righteousness of Christ by faith. Thus the meal which unites must primarily be a sacrifice of praise and thanksgiving to Almighty God for all his grace towards mankind.

It follows from this that a true eucharist will not be the preserve of any one particular church organisation or tradition, for "the wind blows where it will, and you hear the sound of it, but you do not know whence it comes or whither it goes" (John 3:8). As this book has aimed to show, the wind of God's grace has blown in some very strange and unlikely places during the past two thousand years. It has by no means been restricted to the Roman Catholic or Orthodox churches, or the "mainline churches of Western Protestantism". Sometimes it has been distressingly absent from large areas of these communions and has been more in evidence in scattered groups of harassed and persecuted "heretics". Now to the discomfiture and bewilderment of some extreme evangelicals who have become hardened and dry in their own tradition the wind of the Spirit is blowing freely again in the ancient churches of catholic Christianity. "The wind blows where it wills."

(ii) A true eucharist must express the priority of faith

Of course God's gracious action precedes man's believing response. Sometimes sacramentalists have needed to remind evangelicals of this fact. But grace becomes effective only in the outworking of faith. All too often the sacraments have become instruments of superstition, their alleged effectiveness being closer to the working of magic than of grace. But the Gospel always brings a challenge to repent and believe, and a sacrament which "proclaims the Lord's death" and says, "This is the new covenant in my blood," must always focus attention on this fact. Thus in the eucharist the Word must be preached, the great centralities of incarnation, atonement and resurrection must be declared, and a plethora of actions, gestures and ceremonies which might obscure these great truths must always be shunned.

(iii) A true eucharist must give expression to the church as the body of Christ

At the cross Christ sealed the New Covenant in his blood. Those included in this covenant "are a chosen race, a royal priesthood, a holy nation, God's own people, that you may declare the wonderful deeds of him who called you out of darkness into his marvellous light" (1 Peter 2:9). Thus, outside the church there is no salvation, for commitment to Christ must involve commitment to his people. That the church is the body of Christ was the great rediscovery of the liturgical movement, and it followed, quite rightly, that the eucharist was not something which was said but something which is done. The eucharist is thus not an individualistic affair wherein Christians "make their communion" but is a corporate activity of the whole church in which every member of the body of Christ has a part to play.

Unfortunately, the liturgists did not press their discovery far enough and limited the activity of bishop, priests and people to ritualistic actions alone. Thus the action of bishop was to preside, the action of priest was to administer, and the action of the people was to present the offertory. In their enthusiasm for this traditional separation of priests and people, the liturgists forgot that in the church all are priests, that in the church's worship each one may have "a hymn, a lesson, a revelation, a tongue, or an interpretation" (1 Corinthians 14:26), that all may minister "one by one, so that all may learn and be encouraged" (1 Corinthians 14:31). It has taken charismatic renewal to begin to explore the full extent of the church's activity in the eucharist, wherein an extended Peace may provide opportunity for counselling and prayer, where the ministry of healing and the laying-on-of-hands may follow the distribution of the bread and wine, and where a period of spontaneous praise may anticipate the eternal worship of Heaven.

Through the church God continues to speak to the world (see 1 Peter 2:9), and when the church, quickened and empowered by the Holy Spirit, thus celebrates the eucharist, it will be equipped and strengthened for its ongoing work of proclamation and call. Not only so, but in its whole ministry and worship, unbiblical emphases will be corrected and neglected elements will be restored, for the Spirit is the Spirit of truth and his work in the church can never contradict his word in the Bible. And as the Spirit is given freedom to work in the church, so that unity of God's people for which Jesus prayed in John 17 will begin to become a reality. "Because there is one bread, we who are many are one body, for we all partake of the one bread" (1 Corinthians 10:17).

The Jews in Jesus' time believed that when the Messiah came he would inaugurate the Kingdom of God with a great banquet at which all his faithful people would sit down and eat. The eucharist is the foretaste of that banquet. "Christ, our paschal lamb, has been sacrificed. Let us, therefore, celebrate the festival, not with the old leaven, the leaven of malice and evil, but with the unleavened bread of sincerity and truth" (1 Corinthians 5:7, 8).

CHAPTER EIGHT NOTES

1 – *The Evangelical Magazine*, November 1970, p. 4.
2 – *Christian Worship*, N. Micklem, p. 243.
3 – J. Calvin, *Institutes of the Christian Religion*, Bk. 4. xiv. pp. 4–5.
4 – E. L. Mascall, *Corpus Christi*, p. 194.
5 – *The Evangelical Magazine*, November 1970, pp. 10 & 11.
6 – Friedrich von Hügel, *Selected Letters*.
7 – S. F. Winward, *The Reformation of our Worship*, p. 54.
8 – *Theological Renewal*, October 1978, p. 31.
9 – *ibid.*, ditto, p. 32.
10 – *Testimony Magazine*, October 1973.

SELECT BIBLIOGRAPHY

Raymond Abba, *Principles of Christian Worship*, Oxford University Press, 1957.
Thomas Aquinas, *Summa Theologia*, Eyre & Spottiswoode, 1964.
Gustav Aulen, *Eucharist and Sacrifice*, Oliver & Boyd, 1958.
D. M. Baillie, *The Theology of the Sacraments*, Faber, 1957.
Roland H. Bainton, *Here I Stand — a Life of Martin Luther*, Hodder and Stoughton, 1951.
G. R. Balleine, *A History of the Evangelical Party in the Church of England*, Longmans, Green & Co., 1933.
John M. Barkley, *The Worship of the Reformed Church*, Lutterworth, 1966.
Louis Bouyer, *Life and Liturgy*, Sheed & Ward, 1956.
John C. Bowmer, *The Sacrament of the Lord's Supper in Early Methodism*, Dacre Press, 1951.
Yngve Brilioth, *Eucharistic Faith and Practice: Evangelical and Catholic*, SPCK, 1930.
E. H. Broadbent, *The Pilgrim Church*, Pickering & Inglis, 1974.
Colin Buchanan, *Encountering Charismatic Worship*, Grove Books, 1977.
Colin Buchanan et al., *Growing Into Union*, SPCK, 1972.
Colin Buchanan, *Liturgy for Communion: The Revised Series 3 Service*, Grove Books, 1979.
ed. Colin Buchanan, *Modern Anglican Liturgies*, 1958–68, Oxford University Press, 1968.
Colin Buchanan, *The End of the Offertory — an Anglican Study*, Grove Books, 1978.
Colin Buchanan, *What Did Cranmer Think He Was Doing?* Grove Books, 1976.
John Calvin, *Institutes of the Christian Religion*, James Clarke, 1957.

Julian Charley, *The Anglican-Roman Catholic Agreement on the Eucharist*, Grove Books, 1971.

Larry Christenson, *A Message to the Charismatic Movement*, Bethany Fellowship, Inc.

W. K. Lowther Clarke, *The Prayer Book of 1928 Reconsidered*, SPCK, 1943.

F. R. Coad, *A History of the Brethren Movement*, Paternoster, 1968.

A. O. J. Cockshutt, *Religious Controversies of the Nineteenth Century*, Methuen, 1966.

Collected Writings of J. N. Darby, Stowe Hill Bible & Tract Depot, 1900.

Thomas Cranmer, *True and Catholic Doctrine and Use of the Sacrament of the Lord's Supper*, Chas. J. Thynne, 1907.

J. D. Crichton, *Christian Celebration: The Mass*, Geoffrey Chapman, 1971.

G. J. Cuming, *A History of Anglican Liturgy*, Macmillan, 1969.

Geoffrey J. Cuming, *Essays on Hippolytus*, Grove Books, 1978.

Geoffrey J. Cuming, *Hippolytus: A Text for Students*, Grove Books, 1976.

Merle d'Aubigne, *The Reformation in England*, Banner of Truth Trust, 1963.

Horton Davies, *The Worship of the English Puritans*, Dacre Press, 1948.

Horton Davies, *Worship and Theology in England*, Princeton University Press, 1961–75.

Gregory Dix, *The Shape of the Liturgy*, Dacre Press, 1943.

C. W. Dugmore, *The Mass and the English Reformers*, Macmillan, 1958.

John Fenwick, *The Eastern Orthodox Liturgy*, Grove Books, 1978.

P. T. Forsyth, *The Church and the Sacraments*, Independent Press, 1910.

J. R. Green, *A History of the English People*, Macmillan, 1880.

David Gregg, *Anamnesis in the Eucharist*, Grove Books, 1976.

R. P. C. Hanson, *Eucharistic Offering in the Early Church*, Grove Books, 1979.

ed. A. G. Hebert, *The Parish Communion*, SPCK, 1937.

R. C. D. Jasper and G. J. Cuming, *Prayers of the Eucharist, Early and Reformed*, Collins, 1975.

Joachim Jeremias, *The Eucharistic Words of Jesus*, SCM Press, 1970.

Josef Jungmann, *The Early Liturgy*, Darton, Longman & Todd, 1960.

J. A. Jungmann, *The Eucharistic Prayer*, Anthony Clarke, revised ed. 1978.

J. N. D. Kelly, *Early Christian Doctrines*, Adam & Charles Black, 1960.

F. D. Kidner, *Sacrifice in the Old Testament*, Tyndale Press, 1952.

Theodore Klauser, *A Short History of the Western Liturgy*, Oxford University Press, 1969.

E. J. Koenker, *The Liturgical Renaissance in the Roman Catholic Church*, University of Chicago Press, 1954.

W. H. Mackean, *The Eucharistic Doctrine of the Oxford Movement*, Putnam, 1933.

J. T. McNeill, *The History and Character of Calvinism*, Oxford University Press, 1954.

E. L. Mascall, *Corpus Christi*, Longmans, 1953.

E. L. Mascall, *Recovery of Unity*, Longmans, 1958.

B. A. Mastin, *Jesus Said Grace*, Scottish Journal of Theology, Vol. 24, No. 4, 1971.

Stephen Mayor, *The Lord's Supper in Early English Dissent*, Epworth Press, 1972.

N. Micklem, *Christian Worship*, Clarendon Press, 1950.

C. F. D. Moule, *Worship in the New Testament*, Grove Books, 1977.

ed. J. I. Packer, *Eucharistic Sacrifice*, Church Book Room Press, 1962.

ed. J. I. Packer, *Guidelines*, Falcon Books, 1967.

G. R. Potter, *Zwingli*, Cambridge University Press, 1976.

Joseph Powers, *Eucharistic Theology*.

A. M. Ramsey, *Durham Essays and Addresses*, SPCK, 1956.

J. Ernest Rattenbury, *The Evangelical Doctrine of Charles Wesley's Hymns*, Epworth Press, 1941.

W. H. Rowdon, *Origins of the Brethren*, Pickering & Inglis, 1975.

ed. C. Lancelot Sheppard, *The New Liturgy*, Darton, Longman & Todd, 1970.

Kenneth W. Stevenson, *Gregory Dix — Twenty-Fives Years On*, Grove Books, 1977.

A. M. Stibbs, *Sacrament, Sacrifice and the Eucharist*, Tyndale Press, 1951.

A. M. Stibbs, *The Finished Work of Christ*, Tyndale Press, 1954.

A. M. Stibbs, *The Meaning of the Word "Blood" in Scripture*, Tyndale Press, 2nd ed. 1954.

The Lord's Supper — a Baptist Statement, Carey Kingsgate Press, 1961.

Jean M. R. Tillard, *Roman Catholics and Anglicans: The Eucharist*, One in Christ, July 1973.

Jean M. R. Tillard, *What Priesthood Has The Ministry?* Grove Books, 1973.

Simon Tugwell *et al.*, *New Heavens? New Earth?* Darton, Longman & Todd.

Leonard Verduin, *The Reformers and Their Stepchildren*, Paternoster, 1964.

Stephen Winward, *The Reformation of our Worship*, Carey Kingsgate Press, 1964.

Works of John Owen, Banner of Truth Trust, 1965.

Frances M. Young, *Sacrifice and the Death of Christ*, SPCK.

INDEX

Act of Uniformity 1559, 110
Act of Uniformity 1662, 109, 114
Agreed Statement on the Eucharist, see Anglican-Roman Catholic International Commission
Alcuin, 71
Alternative Services, 119f.
Ambrose, Bishop of Milan, 62f.
Anglican-Roman Catholic International Commission, 158–61
Anglicanism, see Church of England
Apostolic Succession, 50, 66, 89f., 111f., 128ff., 132f., 137f., 151, 157, 163f., 177f.
Aquinas, Thomas, 75–9, 81, 90, 118, 172
Aristotle, 75–7, 118
Augustine, Bishop of Hippo, 75, 78
Baptists, 110, 114ff., 129, 138, 156
Baxter, Richard, 113
Berengar of Tours, 70, 80
Bilney, Thomas, 104
Bohemian Brethren, 100, 124
Book of Common Prayer, 105, 107ff., 110, 114, 132, 145f., 149
Borlase, Henry, 137
Bunyan, John, 116f.
Calvin, John, 44, 75, 87f., 99–103, 105f., 151, 169
Cambridge Camden Society, 132
Carlstadt, Andreas, 94
Catholic Emancipation Act 1829, 129
Charismatic Movement, 43, 161–4, 168, 176, 178ff., 184
Charlemagne, 71
Chrysostom, John, 63f.
Church Councils,
   Council of Constance, 81
   Fourth Lateran Council, 70
   Council of Rome, 70, 76f.
   Second Vatican Council, 143, 158
   Council of Trent, 75, 118, 142, 167, 169
Church of England, 24, 33, 44, 100, 104–17, 123–40, 145–50, 155–61, 177, 179
   Broad Church Party, 145
   Catholic thought in, 33f., 44, 129–35, 140, 145–50, 170f.
   Evangelical thought in, 145, 149f., 170f.

Evangelical Revival, 123–9, 133f., 135, 140
   Liturgical Commission, 56f.
Church of Rome, 15, 21, 24f., 44, chapters 3, 4 *passim*, 87–93, 96, 99f., 108ff., 118–20, 130f., 133, 137f., 140, 142–5, 155f., 158–161, 169, 172f., 176f., 182
Clayton, John, 124
Clement, Bishop of Alexandria, 48
Congregationalism, 112, 115, 129, 175
Constance, Council of, see Church Councils
Constantine, 59f.
Consubstantiation, 90
Coptic Church, 180
Corpus Christi, see Reservation
Counter-Reformation, 118f.
Cranmer, Thomas, 103–10, 131
Cyprian, Bishop of Carthage, 58, 61
Cyril, Bishop of Jerusalem, 61ff.
Darby, John Nelson, 135–40
Deutsche Mass, 92
Didache, 47ff.
Dissent, 110–17, 123, 151f.
Dix, Gregory, 56, 60, 146–9, 152f.
Ecumenical Movement, 154–61
Epiclesis, 44, 144, 146, 150, 163f., 178ff.
Eucharistic Prayer, 47ff., 52, 55, 57, 63, 102f., 146f., 149f., 152, 178
Evangelicals and evangelicalism, 33, 84, 125f., 128, 135, 144, 155f., 168, 170, 177, 183. See also Church of England, Evangelical thought in
Farel, Guillaume, 99
Fourth Lateran Council, see Church Councils
Free Churches, see Nonconformity
Frere, Bishop, 109
Froude, Hurrel, 129
Gnosticism, 49ff., 53, 58, 69, 96, 180
Great Schism, 62
Groves, Anthony Norris, 136, 140
Hippolytus, 53–8
Holy Club, 124f., 128
Hooker, Richard, 106
House Church Movement, 14, 139, 161
Hus, Jan, 83f., 87, 104, 124
Independents, 114. See also Congregationalism

191

INDEX

Irenaeus, 50, 53, 58, 61, 148
Judaism, chapter 1 *passim*, 32–8, 48f., 58, 174, 184
Justin Martyr, 48, 50, 51ff.
Keble, John, 129–32, 135, 140
Knox, John, 102f.
Lanfranc, Archbishop of Canterbury, 70
Last Supper, chapter 1 *passim*, 172
Latimer, Hugh, 104, 108
Laud, William, 109
Liturgical Movement, 142–54, 161f., 183f.
Lollards, 82f.
Luther, Martin, 75, 84, 87–93, 94–8, 100, 103f., 169
Lutheran Church, 44, 100
Marburg, Colloquy of, 97f.
Mass, 38, 40, 65, 69–75, 81, 84f., 87ff., 91, 94, 96, 104–8, 118f., 133, 140, 142–5, 169
Memorialism, 93–8
Methodists, 124–8, 138, 150, 157, 175, 177, 180
Milan, Edict of, 59f.
Mirk, John, 70f., 77
Montanism, 43
Moravians, 124f.
Moule, Handley, 134
Neale, John Mason, 132
Newman, John Henry, 129–32, 135ff., 140
Newton, Benjamin, 136
Nominalism, 95
Nonconformity, 112, 114f., 117, 136ff., 146, 150, 152ff., 162, 172, 178
Offertory, 36, 52f., 143, 147f., 153, 171, 176, 184
Ordination, see Apostolic Succession
Origen, 48
Orthodox Churches, 14f., 21, 25, 30, 44, 49, 57, 62, 155
Owen, John, 115
Passover, 13f., 16f., 20f., 23f.
Paul, Apostle, 15, 24–9
Paul VI, Pope, 158
Pelagius, 171
Pentecostalism, 14, 155, 161f., 176
Pius XII, Pope, 143
Plymouth Brethren, 135–40, 175
Prayer Book of the Church of England, see Book of Common Prayer
Presbyterianism, 102, 112, 114, 128f.
Puritans, 111–14
Pusey, E. B., 130, 134f., 140
Quakers, 14, 116
Radbert, Paschasius, 69f.
Ramsey, Michael, Archbishop of Canterbury, 147, 158, 171
Real Absence, 98, 105
Real Presence, 44, 62, 70, 77, 80, 90, 105f., 118, 126, 134, 144, 159, 172–6
Receptionism, 103–9
Reformation, 15, 18, 25, 27, 33, 36, 75–84, 87–120, 139, 167, 177
Remanence, 80
Reservation, 60, 73f., 83, 143, 146, 150, 172
Ridley, Nicholas, 108
Roman Catholicism, see Church of Rome
Rome, Council of, see Church Councils
Salvation Army, 14
Second Vatican Council, see Church Councils
Separatists, 110f., 114
Strasbourg Rite, 102
Tertullian, 50
Thanksgiving Prayer, see Eucharistic Prayer
Theodoret, 64
Trent, Council of, see Church Councils
Tractarian Movement, 128–35, 137f., 140
Transubstantiation, 15, 18, 44, 51, 61ff., 66, 69–85, 90ff., 93, 105, 118, 144, 159, 167, 172f.
Tyndale, William, 104
Ubiquity, 90, 95, 100
United Reformed Church, 112. See also Presbyterianism and Congregationalism
Vestments, 52, 60, 72, 123, 125, 132ff., 144, 170
Virtualism, 99–103
Vulgate, 79, 87, 100, 104
Waldo, Peter and Waldensians, 83, 100
Waterland, Daniel, 106
Wesley, John and Charles, 124–8, 175
Whitefield, George, 125
William of Occam, 95
World Council of Churches, 155f.
Wyclif, John, 79–82, 83f., 87, 104
Zürich Rite, 97
Zwingli, Ulrich, 87f., 93–9, 100ff., 105, 116f.